Mary the Mother of the Lord
in the New Testament

Klemens Stock, S.J.

MARY THE MOTHER OF THE LORD IN THE NEW TESTAMENT

Translated by Joseph Chalmers, O. Carm.

EDIZIONI CARMELITANE
ROMA

Copyright © by EDIZIONI CARMELITANE. All rights reserved. No part of this publication may be reproduced, stored in a retrieval system, or transmitted, in any form or by any means, electronic, mechanical, photocopying, recording, or otherwise, without the prior written permission of the publisher.

Cover: *Our Lady of Mercy* - Thessalonic, Greece, 2004.

ISBN 88-7288-090-4
ISSN 0394-7750

© EDIZIONI CARMELITANE
Via Sforza Pallavicini, 10
00193 Rome / Italy
edizioni@ocarm.org

CONTENTS

Preface 7

Introduction 9

I. Mary in the Gospel of Matthew 19
    1. Mary in the genealogy of Jesus (1,1-17) 19
    2. Mary at the service of God (1,18-25) 28
    3. The child and his mother (2,1-23) 33

II. Mary in the Gospel of Mark 39
    1. Jesus' relatives go to him (3,31-35) 39
    2. Jesus returns to Nazareth (6,1-6) 46

III. Mary in the Gospel of Luke 55
    1. The vocation of Mary (1,26-38) 55
       a) Mary of Nazareth (1,26-27) 56
       b) God and Mary (1,28-29) 56
       c) The mother of the Messiah (1.30-34) 62
       d) The servant of the Lord (1,35-38) 66
    2. The meeting of Mary and Elizabeth (1,39-45) 69
       a) Mary and Elizabeth (1,39-41) 69
       b) Mary blessed by God (1,42-44) 73
       c) Mary is blessed and full of faith (1,45) ... 77
    3. Mary praises the greatness of the Lord
       (1,46-55) 80
       a) Mary praises God (1,46-49) 80
       b) Mary and the Holy God (1,49-53) 84
       c) Mary and Abraham (1,54-55) 89

    4. Mary and Bethlehem (2,1-20) 91
    5. Mary with her child in the Temple (2,21-40)   95
    6. Mary and Jesus at 12 years of age (2,41-52).   99
    7. Mary and the public ministry of Jesus
       (8,19-21; 11,27-28) 103

IV. Mary in the Gospel of John 111
    1. The Mother of Jesus at Cana (2,1-12) 114
    2. The Mother of Jesus at the foot of the cross
       (19,25-27) 117

V. Mary in the other New Testament Writings 123
    1. Mary in the newborn Church (Acts 1,14) 124
    2. The Mother of God's own Son (Gal 4,4-5) . 129
    3. Mary, the sign in heaven (Apoc 12,1-6) 138

VI. Mary in the New Testament 145
    1. The images of Mary 145
       a) Matthew: the service of the Virgin Mother 146
       b) Mark: the care of the Mother for her Son.. 147
       c) Luke: Mother and listener to the word of
          God 155
       d) John: Mother of Jesus and Mother of his
          disciples 160
       e) Acts of the Apostles: the Mother of Jesus
          in the Church 163
       f) Paul: the Mother of the Son of God 164
       g) Apocalypse: the Mother as sign in heaven 165
    2. Mary, the Mother of the Lord 166

PREFACE

I have great pleasure to present this little book by Fr. Klemens Stock S.J, the renowned biblical scholar from the Pontifical Biblical Institute. It is a translation of a work initially written in Italian.[1] Fr. Stock himself brought it to my attention when I asked his permission to translate another of his works.[2] On reading his analysis of all the biblical texts relating to Mary, the Mother of Jesus, I was very happy to translate it and make it available to an English speaking public.

Fr. Stock brings a long background of great scholarship on the New Testament to the study and exposition of these biblical texts. Like every excellent teacher he is able to express profound scholarship very simply. Therefore this book can be read with profit by those with a good knowledge of the Bible and those with none. It may be of help to individuals for private prayer or study, or for Lectio Divina groups.

---

[1] *Maria, La Madre Del Signore, Nel Nuovo Testamento*, Edizioni ADP, Roma, 1997

[2] *The Call of the Disciple*, Edizioni Carmelitane, Roma, 2006.

As a Carmelite, naturally I have a great interest in Mary, the Mother of Jesus. I hope that this book will increase your knowledge of God's plan for the world and Mary's place in this plan of salvation.

> Fr. Joseph Chalmers O.Carm.
> Prior General of the Carmelite Order

Solemnity of the Assumption of Our Lady 2006

INTRODUCTION

At the centre of the New Testament there is the good news that Jesus of Nazareth is the Christ and the Son of God (Mk 1,1; Jn 20,31; Rom 1,9; Gal 1,16 etc). Everything else derives from this fundamental reality or is directed towards it. In reference to Jesus, the New Testament speaks also of his mother, Mary. In order to get to know her, we have in the New Testament the most ancient and indeed the only sources. In this book we propose to examine all the texts that speak of her. In this way our knowledge of her will be enriched and placed on a solid foundation.

"All generations will call me blessed"

The interest in Mary and research about her come from the New Testament itself. It is here that we find that extraordinarily audacious announcement: *"From henceforth all generations will call me blessed "* (Lk 1,48).[3] Those are Mary's words in her hymn of praise for the work of God (Lk 1,46-55). She announces that in all ages people will go to her, will regard her destiny with amazement and will recognise her blessedness,

---

[3] All Scripture texts are translated directly from the words of the author in order to stick closely to the point he wishes to make. The translations of the texts are checked back to major biblical translations to ensure accuracy.

the fullness of joy. If this expression is taken literally, from a purely human point of view, it could seem to be exaggerated and pretentious. However, if we look at it from the perspective of history, we can see that even to our own days, it has proven true.

Mary does not only announce that people in the future will be interested in her, but she also stresses the reason: "*Because the Almighty has done great things in me*". These are not personal privileges of Mary, but the greatness of the powerful action of God in her regard will continually direct attention to her and will awaken people's admiration. God chose her and made her capable of being the mother of His own Son; in her the Son of God became human. The reason for the blessedness, which will never cease, is precisely that she is the mother of God's Son. Because of her relationship with Jesus, Mary has a special role, and this is the foundation of why we turn to her.

In his explanation of the Magnificat, Martin Luther writes: "The 'great things' are nothing else than the fact that Mary became mother of God. In this event she received so numerous and so great graces that no one could grasp them. From this comes every honour and blessing for her; from this comes her singular position in the whole human race, elevated above everyone else. There is no other person like her, because she shares a child with the heavenly Father, and what a child! Mary herself cannot name him because of his immense greatness and must limit herself to the fervid exclamation that arises from her heart, because indeed so great are these things that they cannot be expressed or measured. Therefore all her honour can be summed up in a single expression, when she is called 'mother of God'. Speaking of her or having recourse to her, no one can say more sublime things, even if he had more tongues than all the leaves on the trees or the grass of the field, or the stars in the heavens or the sand on the shore of the sea. It is necessary to ponder in one's own heart what it means to be the mother of God."

What are our sources?

Within the New Testament, Mary is mentioned almost only in the Gospels, which speak of her in just a few passages. During the public life of Jesus, about which the Gospels are principally concerned, Mary is very much in second place. She is mostly present in the infancy narratives (Mt 1-2 and Lk 1-2).

Nowadays the credibility of the infancy narratives is called into question from many points of view. What is related in them is difficult to verify from other sources, and many elements have a rather unusual character. Furthermore, Matthew and Luke refer to different events. Matthew speaks of an angel that appeared to Joseph in a dream (1,18-25), of the coming of the Magi (2,1-12), of the flight into Egypt and the return to the land of Israel (2,13-23). In Luke we find the annunciation to Mary and her visit to Elizabeth (1,26-56), the birth of Jesus at Bethlehem and the announcement to the shepherds (2,1-20), the circumcision of Jesus, his presentation in the Temple and his return to Nazareth (2,21-40), and the visit to the

Temple of the twelve year old Jesus on the occasion of the Passover (2,41-52). These events are not contradictory, but can be linked, though not always easily. According to Matthew, it seems that Mary and Joseph lived in Bethlehem from the beginning, whereas for Luke, they go there only because of the census of Augustus. Luke says nothing about the flight into Egypt. After the presentation in the Temple, Mary and Joseph return to Nazareth as if this had been the obvious thing to do. In Matthew it seems that Joseph wants to return from Egypt to Bethlehem but is persuaded to go to Nazareth only because of fear of King Archeleaus.

To these tensions regarding the representation of events, can be added the presence of extraordinary elements in the stories. According to Matthew and Luke, Jesus does not have a human father but is conceived in Mary by the work of the creative power of God. Important communications are transmitted by angels who act as messengers of God. A star calls the attention of the Magi to the birth of Jesus and leads them on the road from Jerusalem to Bethlehem.

Due to these elements, often the infancy narratives are not accorded any historical value, or only very little value. However since they are the principal sources for knowing Mary, how can we learn something about her that is historically accurate? We must therefore examine the character and the historical value of the infancy narratives.

The fact that Matthew and Luke refer to such different events that are not always easily reconcilable makes it highly unlikely that they knew, or were influenced by, each other. They composed their accounts of the infancy independent of each other and using different sources. However we should also note the points on which they agree. These are from time to time enumerated and evaluated by important commentators on the Gospels as the historical nucleus, which can be taken from the infancy narratives.

Both the evangelists agree on the following points:

1. The mother of Jesus is called Mary and is a virgin.
2. She is engaged to a man named Joseph, who is descended from King David.
3. Jesus is conceived by the power of the Holy Spirit and so Joseph is not his biological father.
4. When Jesus is conceived, Mary is promised in marriage to Joseph but they have not yet come to live together.
5. When Jesus is born, Mary is already living with Joseph.
6. Jesus was born at Bethlehem of Judah when Herod was king.
7. Jesus also pertains to the house of King David.
8. Jesus grows up in Nazareth, in Galilee.

These points in which Matthew and Luke agree independently one from the other show that they did not compose their accounts in a completely free manner but that they have taken elements from the tradition of historical events. This is not meant to suggest that only the above-mentioned points are historically verifiable. They constitute a nucleus of facts to which can be added many more points. When the presentation of the evangelists is not contradicted by evident truth, we should give some consideration to the possibility that it may be historically true.

Among the points on which Matthew and Luke agree is the virginal conception of Jesus. He had no human father and was conceived by the power of the Holy Spirit. If someone states that Jesus entered the world normally and that Joseph was his biological father, this flies in the face of what Matthew and Luke explicitly declare and what we recite in the Creed: "born of the Virgin Mary". It is not possible to produce an historical proof against the affirmation of the evangelists or to prove the paternity of Joseph. However, one can base objections to the historical veracity of the infancy narratives on the common human experience and one also can be simply convinced that a virginal conception is impossible or absurd.

That is contradicted by the fact that, with regard to the conception without a human father, it is said in Luke's Gospel, "*to God nothing is impossible* " (1,37), and also, "*the Almighty has done great things in me* " (1,49). The text of the Gospel speaks clearly of a virginal conception and refers explicitly to the unlimited power of God. Whoever denies the virginal conception, goes against the affirmations of the Gospel and at the same time makes certain affirmations about God. Consciously or not, such a person claims that God has no such power or no reason to work in such an extraordinary way.

It should be noted that this extraordinary action of God is not arbitrary and spectacular, but corresponds to the intimate meaning of the coming of Jesus. The fact that Jesus did not have a human father, but has God alone as his Father, corresponds to his unique filial relationship with God. The fact that he does not proceed from a normal human procreative relationship but owes his existence to the particular creative work of God shows that humanity cannot produce of itself its own Saviour and that he comes from God as pure gift. The fact that with Jesus the preceding history of the transmission of life from generation to generation comes to a conclusion, reflects the reality that with him God begins a completely new phase in the relationship with the human race. Through him, God gives to humanity in a new way a totally new kind of life. Through his mother, Jesus becomes truly human, and through her, he remains fully related to humanity. We must not consider the virginal conception in an isolated fashion as a strange and unusual event. We can only do it justice and understand it if we see it in the totality of God's actions and in regard to the coming of God's Son.

The points on which the different infancy narratives agree, suggest that in their essence they are historically correct. This is the case for the extraordinary event of the virginal conception. We can therefore count on the fundamental historical credibility of the infancy narratives, and so we can consider them as reliable sources for knowledge about Mary.

This does not however mean that in the infancy narratives we can find a series of exact data on the origins of Jesus. When parents today communicate the birth of their child, they do so immediately after the birth. They communicate what they know from personal experience and based on precise data. Perhaps they will send a photograph of the baby, indicating the day and hour of its birth, as well as the weight and length at birth. Some attach the imprint of the newborn's hand or foot. It is obvious that the infancy narratives do not belong to such kind of communication.

They were written down many years after the events but they go back to the traditions that are based on the events. The authors did not only know about the birth of Jesus, but also his life including his death and resurrection. The infancy narratives stem from the profound knowledge of the person and salvific meaning of the life, death and resurrection of Jesus, which was given to the primitive Church by the Holy Spirit through its reflection on the whole mystery, along with its reading of the Old Testament. What was transmitted to the Church regarding the earthly beginnings of Jesus is viewed from the perspective of its understanding of the whole mystery. This global understanding of the person of Jesus is not arbitrary or false but is based on the inspired experience of the true and complete reality of Jesus. Therefore it does not falsify its understanding of the origins of Jesus but permits us to know the meaning of his coming into the world in a fuller and more profound way. The infancy narratives offer us knowledge of the origins of Jesus and a valid vision of who he is, of his relationship with God and of his significance for men and women.

Matthew presents to us Jesus as the Messiah and the Son of God, in whom the history of the people of Israel reaches its fulfilment. He is persecuted by his own people and venerated among the pagans. He is under the powerful protection of God and he fulfils his task of reconciling Israel and the whole of humanity with God and binding them forever to God. Luke presents broadly the same image of Jesus. He is the Messiah of Israel and the Son of God, who brings to the whole of humanity light, peace and reconciliation with God. While Matthew writes in a very concise and sober manner, Luke tends to be more expressive. He also makes a brief reference to the rejection of Jesus by his own people in his infancy story, but he places much more emphasis on those who receive him with joy and with praise of God. Among these people in the first place is Mary.

This image of Jesus in the infancy narratives corresponds to what we learn from the remainder of the same Gospels. The infancy narratives are a part of the truth proclaimed by the Gospels and can only be put in doubt by challenging the truth of the entire Gospel. However, it is reasonable to ask whether the image of Jesus that emerges clearly from the Gospels taken as a whole, is clear also at the beginning.

Our methodology

We have stated that the infancy narratives offer us trustworthy traditions on the origins of Jesus, in the light of the whole mystery of his person. We base ourselves on the fact that these narratives are part of the truth of the Gospel taken as a whole. It will not be our task to distinguish the understanding of Jesus at each stage: before his birth, at his birth, in the first years of his life etc. We do not want to take the Gospels apart and put them together again following subjective and uncertain points of view. Our attention will be given to the texts of Scripture, as they were composed by the evangelists, linked with the tradition and the understanding of the whole. From this we can become aware of the understanding that the evangelists had of Jesus and of the people who were closest to him, among whom is Mary. For almost two thousand years the Gospel writers have been trusted and we too will trust ourselves to their guidance. We can ask many questions about a number of concrete details to which we will receive no answer. However, if we wish to know who is Jesus, and also Mary, and their profound significance for us, the evangelists are most eloquent. We should not become obsessed by our 21st century questions and then go away disappointed because the Gospels do not answer them. We ought to try to listen in the most open and attentive way possible to the questions they posed, to what interested them and to what they wanted to transmit.

As regards Mary, Martin Luther affirms, in his explanation of the Magnificat: "It is necessary to ponder in one's own heart what it means to be mother of God". Mary, of whom Luke says, "*she stored up in her heart all the things that had happened and she reflected on them*" (2,19), is rightly included in our reflection. The Gospel writers have already done what Luther asks for. The image that they give of Mary comes from their knowledge and reflection, and is aimed at a more profound understanding and knowledge of her. In order to know Mary as she really was, there is no better way than to examine the witness of the New Testament and then to ponder in one's own heart "what it means to be the mother of God".

Chapter I
Mary in the Gospel of Matthew

The evangelist Matthew writes about Mary mostly in the first two chapters of his work, in which he deals with the origins of Jesus. During the public activity of Jesus, Mary is mentioned only twice more. She goes to Jesus along with his other relatives and wants to speak with him (12,46-50). During Jesus' visit to his own homeland, she is mentioned by his neighbours (13,54-58). These two events can also be found in the Gospel of Mark, which speaks of Mary only in this context. When we come to Mark's Gospel we shall examine this more closely.

In Matthew the name of Mary occurs five times to designate the mother of Jesus (1,16.18.20; 2,11; 13,55); nine times she is named simply "mother" (1,18; 2,11.13.14.20.21; 12,46.47; 13,55). Already this is a sign of how important it is for the evangelist that Mary is the mother of Jesus. We will seek to discover what these first two chapters of Matthew can tell us about Mary.

1. Mary in the Genealogy of Jesus (1,1-17)

Every human being has a genealogy, whether he or she realises it or not. No one would exist unless connected, through a long line of people, to the very origins of human life. Every human being carries a mysterious history within that is lost in time, and every person is indebted to the innumerable generations gone before that have passed on life. Existence itself bears witness to such a chain of life. This helps us understand that no individual is an isolated being but is part of a tradition and has innumerable connections with others.

It is very difficult to trace the precise composition of one's family tree and becomes more difficult the further back in time one goes. With regard to genealogies in the Bible, one cannot be sure whether they are intended to indicate exactly from a biological and historical point of view the chain of generations, although they do show the traditions from which the individual has come.

The genealogy of Mt. 1,1-17 (cf. Lk 3,23-38) is preceded by a confession of faith in Jesus as the Christ, in whom is realised the promises made by God to Abraham and David. He is not recognised as the Christ because of a precise historical research uncovering his family tree. It is after his death and resurrection, when he is recognised and believed in as the Christ, that he is inserted into this genealogy. This list does not present a precise succession of generations but does point out the tradition from which the Christ has emerged and which he brings to fulfilment.

Wife of Joseph and Mother of Jesus

At the end of the genealogy, the evangelist writes: *"Jacob was the father of Joseph, the husband of Mary, of whom was born Jesus called Christ* " (1,16). In this verse in which Joseph is indicated as the husband of Mary and she is presented as the mother of Jesus, Mary is mentioned for the first time. Here two relationships are mentioned, which touch her person: she has a juridical relationship with Joseph, with whom she has contracted marriage; she has a natural relationship with Jesus, to whom she has given birth.

The genealogy of Jesus includes 42 men and only 5 women. After the initial phrase, "*Abraham was the father of Isaac* " (1,2), the Greek verb that means "*was the father of*" is repeated 39 times. The father is always named and only exceptionally the mother also. This occurs for the first time in 1,3: "*Judah was the father of Perez and Zerah by Tamar* ". Keeping in mind this constant repetition, at the end of the genealogy it should say: "*Jacob was the father of Joseph, who was the father of Jesus by Mary* ". However the monotonous series of who was the father of who is broken. It is stated "Jacob was the father of Joseph, the husband of Mary". Here a new element is inserted. In the list prior to this, no one is mentioned as the husband of a woman. Also at this point the usual "was the father of" is suppressed and instead a new formula is used: "*from whom was born Jesus, called Christ* ". Mary is the mother of Jesus but Joseph is not the father. The evangelist wants to clearly affirm that Joseph has nothing to do with the birth of Jesus. Therefore he affirms at the end: "*Without him knowing her, Mary gave birth to a son*" (1,25).

Joseph is not connected in a direct and natural way with Jesus. His relationship with Jesus goes through

Mary, his wife. In the following section (1, 18-25), in which Joseph is invited by God's messenger to take Mary as his wife and to give her son the name Jesus, the relationship between Jesus and Joseph is clarified. Joseph is the legal father of Jesus. Through Joseph, Jesus is inserted into the genealogy, which starts with Abraham and includes David.

Inserted into the history of the people of God

Mary, together with her relationship with Joseph and Jesus, is mentioned against the background of the preceding generations. Let us consider the significance of these generations and see how Mary and her son are connected to them, and also see how they are distinguished from them.

Before arriving at the last three people - Joseph, Mary and Jesus - the genealogy contains 44 names, of which 40 are men and 4 are women. If we listen only to the names, the list could seem to be without meaning. If, however, one knows the Old Testament and the history that is connected with these names, then the passage, with which Matthew begins his Gospel, becomes a summing up of the whole history of the chosen people. Behind the first four names - Abraham, Isaac, Jacob and Judah (1,2) - there is the whole history of the patriarchs, which is described in detail in the book of Genesis (Gen 12-50). Similarly the Old Testament speaks in a particular way about the origins of David in the book of Ruth (1,5-6), and of his kingdom in the two books of Samuel. The history of the kings of Judah, listed in Matthew's genealogy in 1,7-11, is described in the two books of the Kings. From the Old Testament we know virtually nothing about the names after the Babylonian captivity (Mt 1,12-15). Even here each name stands for an entire generation, in which the relationship with God was vibrant and which was an essential intermediary for the transmission of life and God's promises.

Two people who stand out in the genealogy are the most important figures of the Old Testament - Abraham and David. God called Abraham and promised to make him a great nation and to bless all the peoples of the earth through him. (Gen 12,1-3).

David also received a promise: *"Your house and your kingdom, thanks to me, will stand for ever; your throne will be secure for ever "* (2Sam 7,16). The genealogy mentions the generations through which the promises are transmitted; which hoped in their fulfilment; which retained vitality through this hope and which, at the same time, without knowing the details, drew ever closer to the fulfilment of the promises.

If we listen to the genealogy attentively and with awareness, we can see that by means of the list of names, it calls to mind the history of God's dealings with the people of Israel. It reminds us also that God chose certain individuals, and acted through them in favour of the people. This is true of Mary; she was chosen and given a task, which is connected to this history. This is also recognised in the Magnificat,

Mary's great hymn of praise (Lk 1,45-55). In Mary's son this history reaches its culmination. God chose Mary to be the mother of the one who would bring this history to its fulfilment.

The Five Women

The genealogy names 39 fathers and only 5 mothers. Along with Mary, these are Tamar, Rahab, Ruth and the wife of Uriah. Why does Matthew name these women? Do they have something in common and what does it mean to place Mary in this company?

Tamar (Gen 38,1-30; Ruth 4,12) is at risk of remaining a widow with no children. She feels that she is being unjustly treated by her father-in-law and she takes an unusual route in order to have children. Rahab (Jos 2,1-21; 6,17.22-25; James 2,25; Heb 11,31), a prostitute of the pagan city of Jericho, runs the risk of being killed together with her whole city. She recognises the God of Israel as the God of heaven and earth (Jos 2,11), and she is saved together with her family. Only Matthew mentions her connection with Salmon (1,5). Ruth is a widow and a Moabite. Her story is told in the biblical book that bears her name. She belongs to the people of Israel and to their God. She follows her mother-in-law, Noemi, to Bethlehem and by means of a number of strange circumstances she becomes the wife of Boaz and is therefore saved from having to live in a strange land as a widow with no children. The mother of King Solomon is not given her name "Bathsheba" in the genealogy, but is called

"Uriah's wife", even though Solomon's conception and birth took place after the death of her husband, Uriah, and her first child with King David. She was then the legal wife of David (2Sam 12, 24-25). In this way Matthew records David's multiple and grave sin with regard to Bathsheba (2Sam 11-12). Solomon, beloved of God (2Sam 12,24-25), was locked in a struggle to succeed David (1Kings 1), and he contributed greatly to his mother's honoured position.

The evangelist, by presenting in the genealogy of Jesus not only the fathers but some of the mothers, wanted to point out that life is not always transmitted in an uninterrupted fashion through legitimate marriages and problem-free births. All these above mentioned women were involved in unusual circumstances that led to their relationship with their husbands. In an unusual way they entered the genealogy. Rahab and Ruth came from paganism, perhaps also Tamar and Bethsheba. This may refer to the fact that the Messiah had to reach out to other peoples as well as to Israel (cf. Mt 2,1-12; 28,16-20), and therefore it is hinted at already in the genealogy. Sin is linked with Bathsheba, and perhaps also with Tamar and Rahab. Christ, who came to free his people from their sins (Mt 1,21), has already been affected by sin in his own background. The way that led to Jesus was certainly not direct and without problems. This shows the power and the wisdom of God's Providence, who takes up everything human into the divine plan of salvation.

All these women are dominated and guided by the desire to live and by means of motherhood they aim at a secure life that is full of meaning. Even though the ways are unusual through which they are involved in the transmission of life leading to the Messiah and to the fulfilment of their own lives, these ways remain within the bounds of possibility for human beings. In the case of Mary, on the other hand, everything comes from God and goes beyond human possibilities. Nothing comes from her own initiative. God chooses her for the task of giving birth to the Messiah, and by means of the divine creative power, creates this new life within her. As for the other women mentioned in the genealogy, so also in Mary's case, life was profoundly marked by giving birth. The unique task that Mary received gives to her life the singular significance of being the mother of the Messiah.

The old and the new life

The sole human act that is recorded in the genealogy is to generate life. There is a constant repetition, 39 times, of the verb that we have translated as "was the father of". Human beings know no other means of transmitting human life. God the creator has given the human race this capacity and has made possible in a way the overcoming of death through the continuation of one's family, people and kind, which goes beyond the lifespan of any individual. Without this capacity we would quickly have become extinct. Along with human life, there would have disappeared also the connection with God, the tradition of this history and the fulfilment of the divine promises. Every form and development of human life presupposes this act of generation, by means of which life is transmitted.

With this whole background, the difference at the end of the genealogy stands out even more. Jesus has no human father and he does not pass on life in the normal way. He has in Mary his earthly mother and he acts always as a son (2,15; 3,17; 11,27; 17,5). He is the Christ (= Messiah), that is the ultimate and definitive king of God's people. He does transmit life. The significance of his mission is that through him, God gives the fullness of life to the chosen people and to the whole of humanity.

Therefore the change at the end of the genealogy brings to our attention the fact that with Jesus, there begins a new kind of life and a new way of transmitting life. This becomes clear not just in the genealogy but also, and principally, through the whole life of Jesus. Through procreation we enter into the human family and receive our earthly existence. For all its beauty and nobility, it is passing and moves inexorably from birth to death. Inasmuch as he is a son of Mary, Jesus is a mortal man, but he has a unique relationship with God and therefore participates in a completely different kind of life that is beyond the human. The fact that he has no earthly father is a reference to his particular relationship with God. With his resurrection, Jesus overcomes death and enters into the eternal life of God. He does not transmit life through the normal process of procreation, but through the call he issues to certain people, when he invites them to become disciples and to participate in his own journey and his own life. That which the first disciples experienced must be transmitted to all people. All must become his disciples and baptism is the sign that they have been welcomed into the life of the Father, the Son and the Holy Spirit (28,18-20). Whoever journeys with Jesus as a faithful disciple, will also participate in his life in the glory of the Father (16, 24-28).

After the coming of Jesus human life continues, characterised by birth and death, but it is no longer enclosed in an unbreakable circle. The circle has been broken; it is now open to a new and unlimited horizon because Jesus participates in the life of God and makes possible our participation also. The fact that Mary did not conceive her son through the normal means of procreation refers to this radical change that has come about. Because she is the mother of the one through whom all people have access to the new and imperishable life, she can be called in a more complete way "mother of all the living", the new Eve (cf Gen 3,20).

2. MARY AT THE SERVICE OF GOD (1,18-25)

In the very first part of the Gospel, Matthew presents Jesus as the Christ, the Son of Abraham and of David. He shows that the whole of history, beginning from Abraham, is orientated towards Jesus and how the coming of Jesus is determined by the plan of God. After many names, comes Joseph as the husband of Mary and she herself as the mother of Jesus Christ. We are given only the names of these three people and

Chapter I: Mary in the Gospel of Matthew 29

their relationship one to the other but nothing more than this.

The following scene (1,18-25) recounts how Joseph overcomes his doubts and welcomes Mary into his house as his wife. With few words, we are told very many things about the three individuals. Mary is present in every statement but there is no mention of her saying or doing anything, nor even or what she felt or thought about the situation. We learn who she is but we are not permitted to listen to her or find out what was going on within her. Mary is a mother through the working of the Holy Spirit. She is the mother of the Saviour, the long-awaited Emmanuel (God with us). She is engaged to Joseph and, together with her child, she comes under his care and protection.

Mother through the working of the Holy Spirit

Mary is engaged to Joseph. According to the Jewish Law, both are bound closely to each other because of these mutual promises. However Joseph is named as the husband of Mary at the end of the genealogy (1,16.19), and Mary is named as the spouse of Joseph (1,20.24). After the engagement, the young woman remained for a year or 18 months in the house of her parents. The young man led her into his house and they began to live together as husband and wife. What Matthew recounts is situated in the interval between the engagement and the living together.

From the beginning Mary is presented as the mother of Jesus Christ but she is mother in a very special sense.

Her son has no earthly father but owes the origins of his existence to the Holy Spirit, to the work of the creative power of God. Joseph is astounded by the fact that Mary is to become a mother and he enters into a crisis. He has nothing to do with the conception of this child. God has intervened and has initiated something completely new in the history of humanity. The genealogy shows that Jesus is closely bound to the history of the people of Israel, of which he is the goal and fullness. Jesus, however, has no earthly father, and is no ordinary member in this chain of generations; he is not the result of this history. Humanity did not produce him itself through human procreation. The Saviour and the Emmanuel comes as a gift of God.

Jesus owes his existence to the creative power of God and emerges from the closest possible bond with God. Therefore he is able to free the people from their sins and to lead them out of the situation of separation from God. He is the Emmanuel: through him and in him, God is with the people and comes into the closest possible union with them. Since he comes from God, Jesus binds the human family to God.

Mary is the woman through whom Jesus comes into the world. God chose her and entrusted her with this task. The salvific action of God reaches out to her and she is completely involved in the work of salvation. Matthew says nothing about how Mary accepted this role and how she actually experienced it. Very simply he says that Mary was the mother of Jesus Christ by the work of the Holy Spirit. The reader is left to reflect on this fact and upon the repercussions for Mary's life.

Mother of the Saviour and of the Emmanuel

The one of whom Mary is mother is given two names. Firstly he is called Jesus (in Hebrew, Jeshua or Jehoshua = the Lord saves), since he has the task of saving his people from their sins (1,21). He also has the name "Emmanuel", to which the Gospel gives the meaning of "God with us" (1,23). Both names are explicitly defined. They are not given without a reason, but they express something essential about the one who bears them. Both names speak of the relationship with God.

The fact that the people find themselves in a situation of sin means that their relationship with God is not right. It means that their behaviour is in contrast to the will of God and that they are separated from God. People can ruin their relationship with God on their own, but they are not capable of re-establishing this relationship by their own power and will. By separating themselves from God, human beings created a distance between themselves and their Creator and the source of life. Far from God and destined for death, they have no hope. Jesus came to set free the people of Israel and the whole of humanity from their sins, and therefore to reconcile them with God and so restore life to them.

All of this is confirmed by the name "Emmanuel". It means that God is with us. God has not abandoned us to ourselves or rejected us, but is beside us and offers us the bond of divine friendship. We are under divine protection and guidance. The love, omnipotence and life of God are with us. All of this comes about with the coming of Jesus. Later he himself will refer to the title, "Emmanuel", when he sends his disciples to all the nations: *"Behold, I am with you all days, even to the end of the world "* (28,20). These are the last words of the Gospel. Until the end of time, Jesus is with us and, through him, God is with us.

As mother of the Saviour and of the Emmanuel, Mary renders a unique service to her people. Through her God gives to humanity the one who leads men and women out of the valley of death and unites them with God, the source of all life.

Under the protection of Joseph

Joseph is not the father of Jesus but he is entrusted with a very important task in relation to Jesus and Mary. He also is taken into God's service. He too is very close to the event through which God gives to humanity salvation and life. Joseph receives the task of taking Mary into his home and giving the name Jesus to the child. In relation to the law and society he is Mary's husband and father to Jesus. He takes on these roles because he is directed to by God. In this way Jesus is legally inserted into the genealogy that goes from Abraham to Joseph (1,2-17). Joseph binds Jesus to the history of Israel and offers a safe space in which Mary can fulfil her task and in which Jesus can grow in order to be able to do his work.

Everything speaks of the love that God has for sinful men and women. God wants to free us from ruination and give us the fullness of life. For this reason God sends the Son, the Saviour, "God with us".

Chapter I: Mary in the Gospel of Matthew 33

For this reason, God calls Mary and also Joseph to serve. Both have been chosen by God, chosen to serve.

3. THE CHILD AND HIS MOTHER

The evangelist recounts how in the Magi the pagans came to the newborn Christ. He tells us that the baby's life was threatened by King Herod, and that God by means of Joseph and Mary took care of the child. In this chapter there occurs five times the expression "*the child and his mother* " (2,11.13.14.20.21). Here Jesus and Mary appear always together and never apart. When the Magi reach their goal, the Gospel tells us: "*They saw the child with Mary, his mother* " (2,11). Joseph must save the child from Herod and he receives this task from God: "*Take with you the child and his mother and flee into Egypt* " (2,13), and he does so immediately (2,14). When it is time to return, he is told: "*Take with you the child and his mother and go to the land of Israel* " (2,20), and once again he obeys to the letter (2,21). The evangelist stresses that the child and his mother were inseparable.

What happens naturally between a mother and child happened also between Jesus and Mary. The baby is totally dependent on his mother, who in turn is bound to him and cares for him untiringly as he grows. Mary and her child are bound together in an intimate communion of life. Matthew, more than all the other evangelists, underlines this time in the life of Jesus and this aspect of his relationship with Mary, when he is a child in need of assistance and she is completely dedicated to his care.

A profoundly human relationship

No baby can produce and ensure its own life. It is completely dependent and in need of care. If a baby is left to its own resources, it will die. In order to live and grow, the baby needs innumerable types of assistance. This does not only refer to the material necessities of life but also the loving care required for happiness. Only with this assistance can a child grow and so become an adult capable of taking care of his or her life.

Like every other person, Jesus began life as a small baby in need of so many things in order to flourish. The fact of having a mother, and being completely dependent on her, underlines with the greatest certainty that he was true man. Jesus shares our life completely from the neediness of the baby to the requirements of a dead man. He walks beside us in every moment of our life, having experienced human life completely. Jesus is "God with us" in the fullest possible sense, without limitations or restrictions. As mother of Jesus, Mary is the proof that he is really and fully a man and that the Son of God did not choose a special kind of life for himself, but he became man even to the ultimate consequences.

A mother cannot have a free and independent existence but is tied in many ways to her child. The needs of her child lay out for her what she must do. She must give herself to her child not just with her hands or her mind but her whole self is involved. Her child depends on her not just for a few hours each day but all day every day.

Chapter I: Mary in the Gospel of Matthew 35

Mary is in this relationship to Jesus. For several years they will share a great deal as he grows and becomes more independent. Jesus does not have this relationship with anyone else, only with Mary.

The homage of the Magi

Matthew recounts that the wise men went to see the newborn child who was threatened by the murderous intentions of Herod. Once again the evangelist shows the communion of life between Jesus and Mary; in joy and in sorrow she is at his side.

When the Magi arrive, the evangelist tells us: *"They entered the house and saw the baby with his mother. Prostrating themselves, they adored him"* (2,11). In this incident Mary becomes aware of the universal significance of her son as these wise men from a far country recognise Jesus as their Lord. Her heart is full of wonder and joy. At one and the same time Mary holds this tiny baby that needs her constant care and attention, and yet she is aware of his mysterious origins. Now she becomes aware that others recognise him too. This child is humanly weak but has a divine task. His natural weakness must not become an obstacle to faith in him and in his mission.

The flight from Herod

In this event both the weakness and the dependence of the child are brought out but we also see the protection of God. Joseph is warned just in time about the mortal danger. King Herod feels threatened by the child; he is worried about his own power and so he wants to eliminate the child. What type of power is it that depends on the killing of a baby for its survival? Flight is the means offered the weak to escape destructive powers. From his infancy we see that Jesus does not meet force with force. He meets the murderous designs of Herod with flight. As an adult he will accept violent death at the hands of those who wield power in the land.

Along with Joseph, Mary also must protect the child. More than the baby, she feels the danger caused by Herod, and the discomfort of the tiring journey to a foreign land. Her union with Jesus brings Mary wonderful and profound experiences but also makes her a participant in many dangers and sufferings.

In the land of Israel

After the death of Herod, Joseph is given the task of bringing the little family back to the land of Israel and once again the child and his mother are explicitly mentioned (2,20.21). The one who has come as the son of Abraham and the son of David must grow up among his own people rather than in a foreign land. Matthew tells us nothing about the longest period of the life of Jesus, all those years spent in Nazareth. During this time Mary is at his side. It is a period that is circumscribed by the simple life of a little village in Galilee. Mary shares with Jesus not only the highly charged events but also the humdrum daily life.

The most ancient representations of Mary, in the catacombs, show her with the child Jesus. She is characterised by the fact of being the mother of Jesus and so of having shared the greatest possible union with him.

Chapter II
Mary in the Gospel of Mark

The evangelist Mark limits his work to the public activity of Jesus and does not speak of his origins. Jesus comes on the scene for the first time when he goes to John the Baptist at the river Jordan (1,9). In the whole of Mark's Gospel we find the name "Mary" once only (6,3) and it is used to designate the mother of Jesus. Two further times she is indicated as "his mother" (3,31.32). Mary appears for the first time when she goes to Jesus with his brothers (3,31-35).

Her name is remembered by the people in the synagogue when they call Jesus "the son of Mary" (6,3), but she does not seem to be with him at this point.

1. Jesus' relatives go to him (3,31-35)

Mark says in 3,31: *"His mothers and his brothers arrived, and standing outside the house, they sent a message calling for him"*. Jesus is surrounded by a crowd of people and he does not take up this invitation. He poses the question about who is really related to him (3,33) and he looks at those who are sitting around him and points to them as his true family (3,34). Then he affirms in a general way: *"The one who does the will of God is my brother, and sister and mother"* (3,35).

The clarification of Jesus

Jesus contrasts the bonds brought about by family relationships with another kind of family, based on doing the will of God. He also affirms that those who are gathered round him and listen to him, are in fact doing the will of God. In this way he implicitly declares that his mother and his brothers, who want to call him and take him back home (cf. 3,21), have a different idea of the will of God.

The ultimate criterion for all behaviour is that one must do the will of God. Jesus puts forward the claim that he knows what God's will is for himself as well as for others. He understands his role as being that of making God known as well as God's will. Whoever wishes to live in communion with him must accept this claim. Whoever does not accept it, excludes himself from communion of life with him. Even the bonds of his natural family must be reinterpreted from this perspective.

Jesus speaks with great clarity and firmness. He admits no exceptions, even for his mother and brothers. For them too, he reveals the will of God through his words and deeds. They too must readjust according to this criterion; otherwise they can have no communion with him.

The preoccupations of his family

In Mk 3,31-35, it is not obvious what is the issue between Jesus and his family. The fact that he is

Chapter II: Mary in the Gospel of Mark

surrounded by a crowd and the family is outside calling for him, may indicate different points of view but not necessarily an open disagreement. We can only understand the issue if we look at the whole scene as reported by Mark in 3,21 and 3,22-30.

In 3,21, we are told, *"His family, having heard this, went to fetch him by force because they said, 'he has gone mad'"*. In this verse it is necessary to clarify above all what the family of Jesus have heard and who it is that is saying he has gone mad.

Often Mk 3,21 is linked with what it immediately follows in 3,20, where it says, *"Jesus went into a house and once again a crowd gathered. It got to such a point that neither he nor his disciples could even eat."* So Mk 3,21 is often explained in the following way: the members of Jesus' family have heard about all this continuous pressure on him and that he does not even have time to eat. This has brought them to believe that he has gone mad and so they go in order to bring him back to Nazareth by force if necessary.

Some elements, however, contradict this interpretation. It does not seem to take into account that the gospel recounted by Mark forms a coherent whole and it seems to attribute to him a series of imprecise elements. The family of Jesus come from Nazareth (cf. 6,1-6); the house in which Jesus is surrounded by the crowd is in Capharnaum (cf. 3,21 and 2,1-2). If that which the family hears concerns this situation, i.e. being surrounded by the crowd and barely having time to eat, then someone would have had to undertake the

42   *Mary the Mother of the Lord in the New Testament*

long journey (for those times) of about 40 km to Nazareth, just in order to tell them. It must also be assumed that the various members of the family all decided to go to Capharnaum together and that when they arrived, they still found Jesus in the same situation, surrounded by the crowd and with no time to eat. Finally it must be assumed that they found Jesus' behaviour so strange that they all assumed he had gone mad and made the decision to take him home with them.

Another interpretation seems to correspond better to the logic of the evangelist and to be more convincing. It is not the family of Jesus who say that he has gone mad, but it is what they hear. They have heard that this opinion is going about among the people. Regarding a similar situation of an opinion concerning Jesus reaching the ear of someone else, Mark refers to it in the same order in 6,14: *"The king heard talk of Jesus, that his name had become famous; it was said: John the Baptist has risen from the dead"* (cf. 6,14-16). Therefore it is not the family of Jesus who judge him to have gone mad, but they hear this opinion and they are naturally very upset. Considering this very serious and dangerous situation, they want to take him back home.

What is hidden under this judgement of Jesus and how dangerous it is, the evangelist shows in the immediately succeeding passage. The Scribes say about Jesus: *"He is possessed by Beelzebul and he expels demons by means of the prince of demons"* (3,22). If others said of him: *"He is mad"*, this does not indicate any intellectual lack but rather is a judgement

Chapter II: Mary in the Gospel of Mark

on the spiritual-religious level. It was also said about Jesus: *"He is possessed by a demon and he is raving"* (Jn 10,20). What the scribes consider to be stupid talk and behaviour, they interpret as being possessed by a demon. The gravity of this accusation is shown by the incisiveness of Jesus' response when he accuses his enemies of sinning against the Holy Spirit (3,23-30). Jesus and his enemies cast up similar accusations to each other. They say that he is possessed by a demon and he accuses them of sinning against the Holy Spirit. Both accuse each other of setting themselves up in total opposition to God. For Jesus this means that he is risking his life. Later on in fact the Sanhedrin will declare him guilty of blasphemy and condemn him to death (14,64). The preoccupation of Jesus' family is not odd but is well founded.

In this interpretation, the description of Mark is coherent, and gives a solid foundation as to why the family of Jesus want to take him back to Nazareth. He presents a clear distinction between the family and the scribes. It is not the members of Jesus' family who put about the idea that he is mad, an idea very close to the other that he is possessed by a demon. The family hear this opinion and are very shaken and so feel moved to action.

Jesus and his family

Regarding the valuation of the situation, there seems to be no difference between Jesus and his family. Jesus is also aware of the increasing opposition to him and the danger that he is courting (Mk 2,1-3.6; 3, 22-30). However his way of dealing with this situation differs from that of his family. When Jesus remained in Nazareth, he did not disturb anyone. His family are moved to action by this consideration. They seem to think that it would be better for him to return home, at least temporarily, where he could live in peace. Why is it necessary to make enemies of the powerful people?

However Jesus recognised that it was the will of God for him to continue his work despite the opposition and the danger. He would betray his mission if he were to interrupt his work and return to Nazareth in order to find peace and safety. He sees that his mission is endangered by the understandable proposal of his family. For Jesus, his mission is a higher value than the bonds of family or even his own life. Whoever does not accept the will of God, which is made known to us through Jesus, cannot be in communion with him. Even his family must accept this and also must accept the dangers.

Jesus and his Mother

In this passage, Mary is presented along with the other members of Jesus' family. Mk. 3,21 speaks in a general way of "his relatives" and this probably includes his mother. In Mk 3,31-35, Mary is explicitly mentioned along with the brothers of Jesus. There does not appear to be any difference made among them. They come together and they act together. The reaction

Chapter II: Mary in the Gospel of Mark 45

of Jesus is directed towards all of them. Mary is not marked out by any particular action or by any special word directed to her by Jesus.

However, it should be noted that she is always mentioned in first place. According to Mk 3,31: *"His mother and his brothers arrived"*. This same expression is used three more times in 3,32.33.34. In his concluding words, Jesus names his mother (3,35). Mary arrives together with the others, but she alone is the mother of Jesus and has this unique relationship with him. The fact that she is named in the first place could make one think that the initiative came from her and that her preoccupation for Jesus was very great. Mary acts like a mother. She has given to Jesus his earthly life and she has cared for him in so many ways. She feels very keenly any danger that he might meet. She acts from her maternal instinct and she wants to protect the life of her son. There is nothing bad or unusual about anything she does. It is a profoundly human and above all maternal preoccupation.

Due to her human preoccupation, she comes into conflict almost necessarily with Jesus. He has another view of life (cf. Mk 8,34-38); for him, true life consists in communion with God, his Father. Only by acting with faith and putting the will of the Father above everything else, even above one's own life, can one remain in communion with God. In this way one has true life. It might appear that Jesus is being very hard and without concern for other people. In a very concise and decisive way, and without any explanation that would soften his words and help the family to understand, he put forward his own vision. Mary is also on the journey of faith and has to learn and mature. Jesus does not tell his mother off but helps her to grow in faith. One could almost add: the one, who has completely understood the vision of Jesus and has allowed it to shape his or her life entirely, could cast the first stone!

Among all the Gospels, that of Mark is the one in which Mary remains mostly in second place, but also in this Gospel she appears consistently as "the mother of Jesus", and her behaviour is determined by her maternal relationship with him. It is particularly important that the evangelist in 3,21 points out the reason for the family's behaviour and of their consequent conflict with Jesus. They want to bring him home because of the general opinion about him and so they are deeply worried about him. Also Mt 12,46-50 and Lk 8,19-21 refer to the family going to Jesus, but they do not give any explanation for their motives, unlike Mk 3,21.

2. JESUS GOES BACK TO NAZARETH (6,1-6)

In Mark's Gospel we are told that Jesus left Nazareth in order to go to John the Baptist to be baptised by him at the river Jordan (1,9), after which he began his public ministry. His family wanted to interrupt this ministry and take him back to Nazareth (3,21). However, he did not accept this attempted interruption and he stated clearly that only the one who does the will of the Father is in relationship with him (3,35).

Now we will look at a passage where Jesus returns to Nazareth but at his own choice, along with his disciples (6,1). Mark makes no reference to a meeting with his family but in the dialogue with the people, there is an explicit reference to his relatives. The evangelist says: "*On the sabbath, he began to teach in the synagogue*" (6,2). It must be assumed that Jesus was in Nazareth before the sabbath and that sometime during his visit the day of rest occurred (cf. Mk 1,32; 6,21.35.47; Lk 4,42; 6,13; 22,14.66). It can be supposed that Jesus would have stayed with his family during this visit. They might have thought that their desire to bring him back home had been realised. However, when he taught in the synagogue at Nazareth, the controversy surrounding him came into his own hometown. The preoccupation of his family must have been all the greater. In Matthew and in Mark, after the scene in the synagogue of Nazareth, Jesus does not speak in another synagogue. As in other cases, his activity causes more and more tension (Mk 3, 1-6; Mt 12,9-14; Lk 6,6-11).

The people of Nazareth and Jesus

Mark sums up the view of the people of Nazareth in regard to Jesus in the following way: "*And they were scandalised at him*" (6,3). In the Gospels, Jesus is rejected more than once but in this case the reasons that the people of his hometown put forward for their rejection are unique. They have to confront two different experiences. With great wonder they witness the wisdom of Jesus' words and the power of his actions. This is completely new for them and they did not expect it from him. His fellow citizens in Nazareth have known Jesus for a long time and so they have developed an image of him. They expect him to follow this image, which is based on their previous knowledge of what he did and of his family. Jesus lived among them as a carpenter, a simple workman. His mother and his other relatives were part of their community. They were, like everyone else, ordinary country people. Nazareth was of no particular importance, and we can see this in the fact that it was never mentioned in the Old Testament or in other ancient writings. Its name appears for the first time in the New Testament; it serves to describe Jesus and it is inseparably linked to him.

Faced with this contrast between what they know of Jesus and what they can see and hear, they could be proud of the fact that a man with such extraordinary power comes from their very ordinary little town and they could have supported him. However, the people come to the opposite conclusion that someone who had lived so long among them until very recently and in such a modest fashion could not possibly have developed so far beyond them in such a brief period of time. Therefore they believed that what seemed to be so extraordinary could not be authentic. They did not know from where he had got such knowledge and power but they would not accept that any of it had any value. They believed that there was no reason for them to be interested in Jesus and certainly they were not prepared to accept that the will of God could come to them through him. They refused to believe in him.

Chapter II: Mary in the Gospel of Mark

The Gospel continually refers to the fact that Jesus was rejected. Usually this happens for "theological reasons", for example Jesus forgives sins and so is considered to be a blasphemer (2,7); he expels demons and is considered to be tied in with Satan (3,22). It is only in Nazareth that Jesus is rejected for "social reasons", at least on the surface. The goal of Jesus is always the same. He wants his message to be accepted and that people make their own the image of God that he preaches. Jesus is accepted by those who follow him; others reject him for various reasons and with greater or less intensity.

The son of Mary

The behaviour of Jesus' fellow citizens shows how discreet he was while he lived among them, and how he inserted himself completely into the life of the modest little village. He is forever connected with this place and is known as Jesus of Nazareth.

This place is also home to Mary and she is well known there. She is mentioned by the people of the village in order to situate Jesus: "*Is this not the carpenter, the son of Mary, the brother of James and Joses and Judas and Simon?* " (6,3). In the parallel passage in Mt 13,55 the villagers ask: "*Is this not the son of the carpenter? Isn't his mother called Mary and his brothers James, Joseph, Simon and Jude?* " Normally a man would be identified as the son of his father, and therefore distinguished from other people who bear the same name (Mk 1,19; 2,14; 3,18; 10,46).

In the Old Testament only Joab, Abishai and Asael are named as sons of their mother, Zeruiah (2 Sam 2,13.18; 16,9.10; 19,23). Zeruiah was a sister of David (1 Chr 2,16). In this instance probably the mother is named in order to stress the relationship with the great king David. Sometimes for the kings of Judah, the names of their mothers are recorded (cf. 2 Chr 20,31: "*Josaphat was the king of Judah .... His mother was called Azubah*"). In this way it was made known which of the many wives of a king had produced the successor.

We have to ask ourselves why the people of Nazareth should name Jesus in this very unusual way, as the son of Mary. Some think that this was a way of discrediting Jesus or that the people only knew his mother and so Jesus was of indeterminate origin. This interpretation cannot be excluded, even though there is no biblical proof for it. Others believe that it is a reference to the virginal conception of Jesus, who had no earthly father. However it is difficult to believe that the people of the village really thought that as they try to point out just how ordinary he is. This could of course be the opinion of the evangelist, who never mentions Joseph as the husband of Mary. The question of the people is clearly determined by the desire to express in the clearest possible way Jesus' connection with Nazareth and his being very ordinary. In this passage there is no attempt to distinguish him from someone else of the same name by adding the name of his father. Since the people name Jesus as the son of Mary, it must be supposed that Joseph has already died while Mary still lives in Nazareth. She seems to have belonged to this village for a lengthy period of time

Chapter II: Mary in the Gospel of Mark

and so it is through her that Jesus is deeply connected with Nazareth, and through her that he is always connected with his own country.

The brothers and sisters of Jesus

In 3,31-35, Mark mentions the mother and brothers of Jesus. The people of Nazareth mention their names: James, Joses, Judas and Simon and they also mention the sisters of Jesus (6,3). They all live in Nazareth, and this fact once again points out that Jesus cannot be an important person since all his family comes from this insignificant little place.

Always the question is raised about what is the relationship between Jesus and his brothers and sisters. After the birth of Jesus, who is conceived virginally, did Mary have a normal marriage with Joseph and give birth to other children? Are the brothers and sisters of Jesus the sons and daughters of Mary? To this question the Gospels do not give an explicit answer. However the Gospels do not contain anything that would contradict the tradition of the primitive Church, according to which, Jesus is the only son of Mary (cf. Lk 2,41-52; Jn 19,25-27), and that she was always a virgin.

The Gospels speak of the brothers and sisters of Jesus but they never speak of any other sons and daughters of Mary. If one believes that they mean the same thing, one goes beyond the text of Scripture and draws a conclusion. It may seem obvious but it is not a necessary conclusion. The terms "brothers" and "sisters" normally mean people who share the same parents but according to Holy Scripture, they may also refer to other close relatives (cf. Gen 13,8; 14,14; 24,48 etc). In 15,40 Mark mentions, among the women who followed Jesus from his activity in Galilee and who stand at the foot of the cross, *"Mary of Magdalene, Mary the mother of James the younger and Joses, and Salome"* (cf. 15,47; 16,1; Mt 27,56). The sons of the second named woman have the same names as those of the first two brothers of Jesus (6,3). She comes from Galilee, is close to Jesus and is distinct from the mother of Jesus. The evangelist does not affirm explicitly, but that is not a contrary argument, that this woman is the mother of the first two brothers of Jesus. If that be the case, then they are not brothers of Jesus in the strict sense.

From a linguistic point of view one cannot answer the questions about the relationship between Jesus and his brothers. However, as we have already said, these passages can be perfectly reconciled with the conviction of the primitive Church that Jesus is the only son of Mary. Adhering to this conviction and understanding, the New Testament from that point of view is dependant upon how one understands the task and position of Mary, based on the Scriptures. Whoever, contrary to the explicit words of Matthew and Luke, does not recognise the virginal conception of Jesus, and believes that he is the natural son of Joseph and Mary, will of course have no problem attributing to the couple more children. However if Mary became a mother by the work of the Holy Spirit and, as the servant of the Lord, dedicated herself completely to the task of being the mother of the Son of God, she therefore adhered completely to the Lord and was consecrated to his service. The one who recognises the virginal conception as real, cannot view it as a momentary event that simply substitutes for the procreative act without leaving any effect on the person and on her life. This was a profound encounter with God, and an experience of being called and given an important task. This encounter with the power of God must mark the whole person. To the Virgin Mary, God gave the task of being the mother of His own Son. It can only follow from this that Mary remained a virgin and fulfilled her role, dedicating herself completely to God.

Rejection by his homeland and family

When the people of his own town reject him, Jesus responds with this observation: "*A prophet is not despised except in his own country, by his relatives and family* " (6,4). This is particularly detailed in Mark's Gospel, whereas Matthew has only "*in his own country and among his own family* " (Mt 13, 57), and Luke has "*no prophet is accepted in his own country* " (Lk. 4,24).

By means of these words, Jesus demonstrates the authenticity of his mission, because, like all true prophets, he too has been rejected by his own people. This affirmation also has a proverbial and global character. It says nothing about the intensity of the rejection and makes no comment with regard to anyone in particular. Therefore it cannot be applied in a blanket fashion to everyone in the same way and it need not necessarily include the mother of Jesus.

The Gospel shows us different forms and grades of rejection. The real enemies of Jesus reject him completely and put him on the side of the demons (3,22) and they want to kill him (3,6). The people of Nazareth do not accept him, but according to Mark, they do not adopt any other measure against him (cf. Lk 4,29-30 for a more extreme reaction). The attitude of Jesus' family is shown by their desire to take him home (3,21.31-35). They have doubts about his work because what he is doing is leading him into grave danger. Even the disciples, who left everything to follow Jesus (10,28), are very confused on his account and they abandon him when he falls into the hands of his enemies (14,27-31.50). That which characterises Jesus - his humility (he comes from Nazareth!), his non-violent behaviour, and his being threatened, all of this is a cause of scandal to everyone. Mark brings out particularly the fact that a full identification with Jesus and following him unconditionally, matures gradually after a long process of purification. It is only possible to be a mature follower of Jesus after his resurrection. Mary is not exempt from this process but she participates in it in her own way.

CHAPTER III
MARY IN THE GOSPEL OF LUKE

In the whole of the New Testament the evangelist Luke is the one who writes in the most detailed manner about the mother of Jesus. He uses her name "Mary" 12 times (1,27.30.34.38.39.41.46.56; 2,5.16.19.34), always in the infancy narrative. She is also referred to 7 times as "the mother of Jesus" (1,43; 2,33.34.48.51; 8,19.20) and 5 of these are in the context of the infancy narrative. Also in Luke, during the public activity of Jesus, Mary is not in evidence.

In a first lengthy passage (1,26-56), Luke describes how Mary is called to become the mother of the Lord (1,26-38) and how both Elizabeth and Mary herself react to this call (1,39-56). Mary is present of course when the birth of Jesus is announced (2,1-20), and also at his circumcision and at the presentation in the Temple (2,21-40), and in the visit of the twelve-year-old Jesus to the Temple (2,41-52). When Jesus makes an appearance in the synagogue at Nazareth, Mary is not mentioned (4,16-30). On one occasion she goes with the brothers of Jesus to him (8,19-21), and once she is called blessed by a woman, without however being named (11,27-28).

1. THE VOCATION OF MARY (1,26-38)

When we recite the "Hail Mary", we use the very words of the New Testament in the first part. We use the words that the angel spoke to Mary: "*Hail, full of grace, the Lord is with you* ", and then the words of her cousin Elizabeth, "*Blessed are you among women, and blessed is the fruit of your womb* ". These expressions are so fundamental and so rich in content that they are repeated over and over in the Rosary and they form the basis for the contemplation of the mysteries of salvation and for the requests that follow in the second part of the prayer.

The original context for the salutation of the angel in Lk 1,26-38 is the passage of the Gospel in which Mary receives her life's task and is called to be the mother of the Son of God. The evangelist presents Mary and the circumstances of her life in a concise way. This is the situation in which she receives and accepts her vocation, and therefore is also the corner stone for the infancy narratives and for the stories of the adolescence of Jesus (1,26-27). In his salutation the messenger communicates what is God's relationship with Mary (1,28-29). Then he goes on to speak of the task for which God has destined her (1,30-34); and finally the angel encourages Mary by reminding her that it is the power of God that will make her capable of fulfilling her role (1,35-38). Mary hears the message of God through the angel, reflects on it, questions, and once everything is clarified for her, she gives her consent. We will examine these passages in order to get to know this call that was given to Mary.

a) Mary of Nazareth (1,26-27)

In this introductory part, we shall try to get to know where Mary lived and what were the circumstances of her life. We learn from the text that she was a virgin engaged to be married.

Nazareth in Galilee

With the initial statement: *"In the sixth month, the angel Gabriel was sent by God"*, the evangelist shows that everything comes from God, who sends the messenger. The messenger communicates God's plan. The initiative always comes from God. The following statements correspond to what one might find in an identity card or something of the sort: name, family and where she lives.

The place is Nazareth in Galilee, which is a mountainous region in the north of Palestine. They spoke a dialect that was unmistakeable in Jerusalem (Mt 26,73) and there the people from Galilee tended to be looked down upon (Jn 7,41.52). To come from Galilee was not esteemed highly by the city people. Nazareth was an insignificant village of country folk, and even the surrounding villages did not give it much consideration (Jn 1,46). Nazareth is never mentioned in the Old Testament or in other ancient Jewish literature. It was brought out of complete obscurity and isolation for the first time by this visit of the messenger of God. It's greatest natural treasure, which still exists to this day, is a spring of water. The archaeological digs to prepare for the building of the new church of the Annunciation in the village, have allowed us to discover much about the conditions of life in ancient Nazareth. Some caves in the mountain served in part as dwellings. Cereals were kept in areas hollowed out from the rocks, as were the stores for grapes for wine and olives for oil. There were hand mills, used by the women, who would sit before day break and grind out the flour for the daily needs. The life was very simple and every family had to struggle for its daily bread. Mary lived in this humble and poor situation. She was a country girl. The parables that Jesus used show that his background was also village life. He also came from the countryside and he was always linked to the village where he grew up, being known as Jesus of Nazareth. This was the village where his mother came from.

A virgin promised in marriage

Twice the evangelist affirms and underlines that Mary is a virgin, a young unmarried woman, but she is already connected in a stable way to a man by being promised in marriage to him. The man was named Joseph and he belonged to the house of David. In those days the engagement was more than a simple promise. By means of the engagement, the marriage was already announced in a way that bound the couple. The girl remained for another year in the house of her parents, and then the man took her to his own house where they began to live a normal married life. Mary received the message from God during the time of the engagement and before the marriage had officially taken place. According to the habitual age for a girl to be engaged, Mary would have been about thirteen years old. Even at this age very important choices had been made in her life. Mary was at the very beginning of adulthood and she had a definite position within the community in the village. She was considered as Joseph's wife, even though they had not begun to live together. She was

Chapter III: Mary in the Gospel of Luke

under his protection and received his help. Joseph would not be the father of Jesus but he grew up in this family where Joseph was the father and Mary was the mother, and in which Joseph took on the tasks of a good and just father of a family (cf. Lk 2).

Finally the evangelist records the name of this young woman. Like several other women in the New Testament, her name is Mary. She is differentiated from the others by the fact that she is the mother of Jesus. As such she has her own place in the history of the people of God.

The messenger of God goes to this young woman, whose conditions of life are very restricted. He does not take her out of these conditions but he communicates to her what will be, in this very place, the great task of her life, according to what God has ordained.

b) God and Mary (1,28-29)

The evangelist described earlier the conditions of life of Zechariah and Elizabeth (1,5) in a similar way as he does with Mary. With regard to Zechariah and Elizabeth, the evangelist adds: *"Both of them were just in the sight of God and observed totally the laws and prescriptions of the Lord"* (1,6). We do not find a similar affirmation with regard to Mary and her relationship with God and the commandments. However the salutation of the angel communicates God's view of Mary: *"Hail, full of grace, the Lord is with you"* (1,28). The actions or the merits of Mary are not the determining factors but how God looks upon her.

"Full of grace"

The messenger of God does not greet the young woman using her own name "Mary", but instead he calls her *"Full of grace"*. This expresses what God has done in her and what she has become as a consequence. If we expand this very dense expression a little, it means: God has filled you with grace; God has given you grace, made you gracious and pleasing. God has made you beautiful and pleasing in His eyes because His grace and love are poured out upon you! Mary is not worthy of God's love because of anything that she has done or because of her merits. The initiative is all God's. God created Mary in such a way that the divine love and benevolence would be directed towards her; this is part of the mystery and miracle of the divine election. This reality is so characteristic of Mary that the angel does not call her by her given name but instead calls her simply "Full of grace".

Reciting the Hail Mary and calling her "Full of grace", we are bringing to mind this fundamental reality of God's relationship with her. With wonder, admiration and gratitude we should direct our attention towards God who stooped down in this very particular way to this girl from Nazareth and made her worthy to receive the fullness of divine love.

"The Lord is with you"

It is evident that also these words speak of the relationship of God with Mary. God, who is Lord, is

Chapter III: Mary in the Gospel of Luke 61

with her. In the Bible, this expression has a precise meaning. It is generally used when God calls a man to a particular task of service to the people, and assures him of the powerful, effective and efficacious divine assistance. In the same way that Mary receives assurance, so also the messenger of God speaks to Gideon, who must free Israel from the Midianites: *"The Lord is with you, oh strong and brave man "* (Judg 6,12). God does not give someone a task and then abandon him to his own devices, but stands beside him and gives powerful assistance. *"Full of grace "* indicates the very personal relationship between God and Mary. *"The Lord is with you "* refers to a particular task to which Mary is being called and which she must carry out in favour of the people of God. This expression points to the fact that Mary is one of those very important individuals who have been called throughout the course of history to give a great service to the people of God. She must be placed in the same category as Abraham, Moses and David. What precise task will be given her is announced by God's messenger after his initial greeting.

Rejoice!

The first word that the angel addresses to Mary means literally "Rejoice". This expression in Greek (the language in which the Gospels were written) was commonly used as a form of greeting. It is usually translated as "Hail" (the English rendering of "Ave", which was the common greeting in Latin). However, in this context the greeting should be given its original meaning, because regarding the coming of Jesus, the messenger of God always presents himself explicitly as a messenger of joy. To Zechariah the messenger announces: *"You will have joy and delight"* (1,14), and to the shepherds he says, *"I announce to you a great joy"* (2,10). In his most important mission, the angel also presents himself as a messenger of joy: *"Rejoice!"* Everything that he has been given to communicate is a cause of joy.

The first reaction of Mary to the angel's greeting is not joy. She is surprised and frightened but she begins to reflect on the meaning of such a greeting. Joy cannot be imposed. It needs time to grow and develop. Through this process of maturation, it becomes so much more profound and penetrating. The first culminating point of Mary's joy is when she breaks out with the Magnificat and her spirit rejoices for what God has worked in her through divine grace and power (1,46-47). From the very beginning Mary's vocation is placed under the sign of joy. God's benevolent attention is focused on her and she is the recipient of a powerful divine intervention directed towards the salvation of humanity. There could be no more authentic motive nor more secure foundation for an overflowing and unlimited joy. When we recite the Hail Mary or the rosary, we should be moved to joy because of the love of God and God's saving action.

c) The Mother of the Messiah (1,30-34)

Mary reflects on the meaning of the greeting of the messenger sent by God. The evangelist always

Chapter III: Mary in the Gospel of Luke

presents Mary as she who meditates on things that happen and who wants to grasp their meaning (cf. Lk 2,19.51). Mary does not allow the meaning of the word and the action of God escape her; she does not follow her own path blindly and unreasonably. She is present with her whole being to God and she becomes personally involved in what is happening to her. She gives a wonderful example of reflection and contemplation. Furthermore she lives in an exemplary manner the attitude that should characterise the recitation of the rosary: dwell on the mystery, reflect, let oneself be drawn into the mystery and, with Mary, be filled by what God says and does.

"You have found favour with God"

The messenger of God speaks once again to Mary who is reflecting on his earlier words. In the latter part of his greeting (*"The Lord is with you "*), he had indicated that God has destined her for a great task. Now he explains just what this task will be in relation to the whole people of God. First of all the messenger returns to the expression *"Full of grace "*, which is the foundation of God's relationship to Mary. The angel says, *"Do not be afraid, Mary, because you have found favour with God."* (1,30). The grace, the favour, the benevolence and love of God are all poured out upon her. God takes delight in her. Once again we see why the angel could begin his greeting with *"Rejoice "*. For human beings there can be no greater happiness than that of knowing with complete security that the omnipotent God, from whom everything comes and everything depends and in whom one can trust in an unconditional manner, loves them and takes delight in them. Any reason for fear and worry is taken away. Mary can be completely happy with her life and her future. God loves her and is on her side.

To be a Mother

The messenger of God communicates to Mary what her task is to be: "*Behold, you will conceive a son. You will give birth to him and you will call him Jesus*" (1,31). Mary is to become a mother. A child is to enter into her life and by his name, he is already marked out as a unique individual. As for every other woman, maternity will change Mary's life totally. She is given a great responsibility and she is asked for a service that is many-sided. She is asked to give her body and her love in order that this child can come to birth and grow. After the birth, the child depends on the mother for many years before it can be capable of living an independent life. Every human being begins life as weak and totally dependent. Only after a long time, much love and a great deal of help, can a human being begin to live a happy autonomous existence.

The presence of a child and the assistance it needs are severe limitations on the freedom of the mother. She can no longer live as before but must be attentive to the needs of her child and look out for its good. What a mother does for her child is the great model for service to other people or love of others (cf. Lk 9,47-48). The service a mother gives her child without a doubt limits her freedom greatly, but at the same time creates a profound bond, which brings great joy. In this bond, the child grows and develops but so does the mother. She gives a great deal in a hundred little ways but she also receives a great deal from the closeness and the trust of her child. A mother has many worries and her life is restricted in many ways, but she is at the same time rich in many profound experiences.

The King of the people of God

Like every other mother, Mary will take care of her child and will enter into a powerfully close bond. However, she alone is the mother of the one whom God sends to His people as the ultimate and definitive king. The angel says to her about her child: *"He will be great and will be called Son of the Most High. The Lord God will give him the throne of David his father and he will reign forever over the house of Jacob and his kingdom will have no end "* (1,32-33). A just king is the pastor of his people. He must take care that all the people live in peace and have the opportunity for a full life. In Jesus, God gives to the people of Israel, and to all people, a pastor and definitive king, who will never be replaced, but will remain forever. This king will give his life for every individual. With his resurrection, he conquers death and opens up to all people access to eternal life, which never ends and is a sharing in the very life of God. He is king in an incomparable way, because through him is communicated the fullness of life.

God calls Mary to offer to the people this unique service. She is asked to bear and take care of the one through whom God offers the fullness of eternal life. Mary is the mother of the Messiah.

d) The servant of the Lord (1,35-38)

By means of the service that Mary offers God, namely accepting to be the mother of the Messiah, God gives the fullness of eternal life to humanity. Mary asks, *"How will this come about?"* The angel responds: *"The Holy Spirit will descend upon you, and the power of the Most High will cover you with its shadow"* (1,35).

The creative power of God

At the beginning of the story, the evangelist has communicated that Mary is engaged to Joseph, of the house of David. To her question regarding how she is to become the mother of the Messiah, she is not told that it will take place in the normal way through relations with her husband. Joseph is not the natural father of this child. Jesus does not take his origins from a man but directly from the power of the Creator of all things. God brings this child into existence without the co-operation of a man. In his concluding words, the angel stresses that the power of God has no limit and that we must not seek to limit it. The angel says: *"Nothing is impossible to God"* (1,37). In her hymn of praise, Mary refers to what the creative power of God has done in her: *"The Most High has done great things in me"* (1,49). Precisely for this reason she will be called blessed by all generations (1,48). We too are called to recognise the work of the power of God and to take our part in proclaiming the blessedness of this woman who experienced it in herself.

In the Gospel we are not told why Jesus comes into the world in this extraordinary way. The reason is certainly not because the bond of matrimony between a

Chapter III: Mary in the Gospel of Luke 67

man and a woman is somehow unworthy. God, from whom all life comes, has established this as the normal way for human beings to come into the world. However, by means of an extraordinary creative intervention at the beginning of Jesus' life, other realities are revealed. God establishes a completely new beginning. God does not abandon humanity, which had a long history of unfaithfulness and evil, to its own devices. God creates in Jesus the new man, capable of attaining fully a profound relationship with God. Jesus is not the fruit of our human history, but is the pure gift of God. Humanity does not produce by itself its own liberator, but God freely gives us the one who overcomes in himself our state of abandonment to sin and death, and leads us to the fullness of life. Since Jesus, from the first moments of his existence, belongs entirely to God, he is capable of bringing men and women out of the situation of separation from God in which they find themselves, and giving to them communion of life with God. In this way, the last and final king (cf. 1,33) gives to his people the fullness of life.

The Son of God

Since he does not owe his existence to an earthly father, but to the creative power of God, Jesus is in a completely unique relationship with God. The angel makes explicit reference to this consequence when he says: *"The child will therefore be holy and will be called Son of God"* (1,35). Scripture defines "holy" as that which pertains to the Lord. The son of Mary comes from God and so belongs to God, who is bound to him in the closest possible way. By reason of this relationship with God, Jesus is called "Son of God". The fact of being, according to his divine nature, the divine Son of God the Father, means that, according to his humanity, he has no earthly father. God is the only Father of Jesus, and is the only source of his existence. Due to this unique bond with God, Jesus is capable of doing the work, which the Father has given him. Jesus can be the definitive king of the people of Israel, and lead this people to the fullness of life.

The servant of the Lord

By the expression, *"Behold the servant of the Lord, let it be done to me as you have said "* (1,38), Mary makes reference to the task that God has given her. Holy Scripture defines "servant of the Lord" as a man to whom the Lord has given a particular calling and to whom has been entrusted an important service to the people of God. Mary is the only woman in the whole Bible to call herself the servant of the Lord. She is placed alongside the great servants of God, such as Moses, David and the prophets. Mary has been called to a unique service, to be the mother of the Messiah, the Son of God, through whom God will offer to humanity the fullness of life and salvation. Elizabeth says of her: *"Blessed is she who has believed in the fulfilment of the words of the Lord."* (1,45). Mary welcomed the task that was given to her and she carries it out in faith, with an unlimited trust in God. In this way she has become a blessing for the whole of humanity.

When we recite the rosary, we have before our eyes the figure of Mary. It will be a blessing for us, and a

Chapter III: Mary in the Gospel of Luke 69

reason for joy, to be able to meditate attentively, and with gratitude on her relationship with God and her vocation. We can reflect along with her on the saving action of God present in the life of Jesus, and we can take her faith and her reaction to God as a model for our own lives.

2. THE MEETING OF MARY AND ELIZABETH (1,39-45)

Mary learns from the messenger of God that Elizabeth, her relative, has conceived a son, and is already in her sixth month (1,36). Mary goes off to visit Elizabeth (1,39-56). In this meeting the two women express what they are experiencing. First Elizabeth speaks and, full of the Holy Spirit, says what she has been brought to understand about Mary (1,41-45). Then Mary speaks and she exults with joy because of the action of God (1,46-55).

a) Mary and Elizabeth

After all that she has experienced, Mary goes to visit Elizabeth. During their meeting they communicate with each other what has happened; they are filled with the Holy Spirit who moves within them. In their meeting they come to understand more deeply the work of God and they announce it aloud.

Moved by the work of God

The encounter of Mary with Elizabeth does not bring about any new decisive event. The event lets us see that the message of the angel to Mary has become known to Elizabeth and is understood by her. The fact that God has chosen Mary and has made her become the mother of the Messiah, through an act of divine creative power, has such a deep meaning and is of such universal importance that it can only be understood gradually.

God is not content to bring about our salvation but desires that we become aware of this plan and understand it more and more deeply, allowing our hearts to be moved. This is the case above all for Mary. From the very beginning, when the angel greets her, Mary is pictured as reflecting (1,29) and then questioning in order to understand more deeply (1,34), and so she grasps in an initial way what is her task. In the meeting with Elizabeth, Mary takes a further step forward when she expresses in the *Magnificat* how she understands the action of God.

Until now this knowledge has been limited to Mary but what God has accomplished in her is not for her alone but is for the whole of humanity. Therefore this knowledge goes further than Mary. Elizabeth is the first person who is given the capacity to recognise what God has done in Mary but this will carry on to all future generations (1,48). We too must reflect on all that God has brought about in Mary, seeking to understand it always more deeply so that we can be surprised by joy.

Mary's journey

The angel told Mary that Elizabeth was already in her sixth month of pregnancy (1,36). She accepted this

Chapter III: Mary in the Gospel of Luke 71

information as an invitation to go and visit her relative in the mountainous region of Judah. According to an ancient tradition, the place where Elizabeth and Zechariah lived was Ain Karim, to the north west of Jerusalem. This would have been a journey of about 120 km for Mary and would have taken several days.

The evangelist tells us nothing about the journey. There is a poem of Friedrich von Spee, which describes what it might have been like:

The gentle and pure Virgin did not journey alone,
But carried with her the Son of God in the throne of her heart;
A host of angels accompanied her invisibly.
When she left home, she began to pray;
At each moment her lips and her heart were directed towards God;
And she continued her meditation on God
Until her journey's end.

What von Spee writes is not a fantastic invention. He simply applies to Mary's journey what the evangelist has already written about her. After she gave her consent, Mary became a mother by means of the powerful action of God. The Son of God began his earthly existence in her body and grew within her. Mary is no longer alone but carries her child in her body. The attitude of reflection with which she accepted the message of God, continues as she goes on her journey. The long hours of the journey offered to Mary the opportunity to think about what had happened and to deepen her understanding of its significance and importance. She has the opportunity to be alone with her child. Mary is filled with God and with God's work.

The greeting of Mary

From this whole journey and her reflection comes the greeting that Mary would have given to Elizabeth. Previously the evangelist told us about the angel's meaningful greeting to Mary: *"Rejoice, oh full of grace. The Lord is with you "* (1,28), and all the subsequent action flows from this. Now he does not tell us what Mary said to Elizabeth. Whatever it was, the child in Elizabeth's womb leapt for joy, and she herself was filled with the Holy Spirit. The evangelist makes explicit reference to Mary's greeting, *"As soon as Elizabeth had heard Mary's greeting....."* (1,41), and Elizabeth refers to it also, *"As soon as the voice of your greeting reached my ears "* (1,44). Mary's greeting had a powerful effect on Elizabeth and allowed her to understand something of Mary's experience. Through the Holy Spirit, Elizabeth can understand what has happened to her young cousin.

Mary's greeting and the effect it produced show the hidden power of the word. With our words we transmit the spirit within us. Our speaking can be animated by many kinds of spirit: they can transmit a good spirit, joy, encouragement, illumination, or a bad spirit transmitting oppression, capable of demoralising and upsetting. Mary lives in the world into which God's messenger has introduced her, and in which she has fully entered with her consent. With her initial

Chapter III: Mary in the Gospel of Luke 73

reflection and in the days of journey that followed, her spirit becomes more and more attuned to the Spirit of God. Her greeting to Elizabeth comes from this spirit and transmits this spirit.

What God has done in and through her, takes possession of her senses and her reflection. It fills her spirit and is transmitted from her to others.

b) Mary blessed by God (1,42-44)

Elizabeth, full of the Holy Spirit, is able to recognise what God has done in Mary and says to her: *"Blessed are you among women and blessed is the fruit of your womb."* Then full of wonder, she exclaims: *"Who am I that the mother of my Lord should come to me?"* (1,42-43)

"God has blessed you"

The first thing that Elizabeth recognises is what God has accomplished in Mary. *"You are blessed"* means "God has blessed you". The foundation is always the action of God. We can evaluate and venerate Mary in a correct fashion only if we do not consider her in an isolated way but in her relationship with God. The angel spoke in the first place of her connection with God: "Rejoice. God has transformed you by His grace. The Lord is with you". (1,28).

To bless, in the proper sense of that term is the work of God alone, and means to give, maintain, promote, to prosper and to bring to the fullness of life. God is the Lord of life; every creature owes its existence to the Creator. Life is a mystery and leads us to God. By saying, *"God has blessed you among women "*, Elizabeth is saying that God, who is the Lord of life, has caused life to spring up in Mary in a way that He has done in no other woman. Every life depends on God and falls within the rules that God has established in creation. Elizabeth is pregnant and she has experienced in a particular way God's blessing because she is old and, until now, barren. John is her child and Zechariah's. Mary, on the other hand, has become a mother in a way experienced by no other woman, thanks to the singular intervention of the creative power of God.

Elizabeth refers explicitly to the fruit of Mary's womb and recognises that it too is blessed. God has blessed the son of Mary, filling him with life. This will only be fully and finally understood at the end of Jesus' life. By his resurrection he overcomes death and becomes the source of eternal life. Through him, God reveals Himself fully as the Lord of life and bestows the greatest blessing of immortal, eternal life. This is the work of God. Mary co-operates with God to bring into the world the one who will conquer death and reveal the true and infinite life.

"The Mother of my Lord"

Elizabeth recognises her Lord in the son of Mary. She cannot explain why the mother of her Lord has come to her. She understands and recognises the dignity of Mary and knows that she is not on the same level. Mary visits Elizabeth and so she participates in the joy of the coming of the Lord. Jesus is Lord of all, full of power and goodness.

In the most common prayer to Mary, the "Hail Mary", we repeat the greeting of the angel and the first words of Elizabeth. Then we add, "Holy Mary, Mother of God, pray for us sinners now and at the hour of our death". These last words, though they do not come from the Gospel of Luke, do correspond to the spirit of what Elizabeth says. She calls Mary "*the mother of my Lord* "; we use "Mother of God", an expression that has been elaborated later and that reveals a profound understanding of her dignity. Elizabeth is aware that she is not worthy to have Mary visit her and that they are on completely different levels. We too are aware of the great difference between Mary and us since we call her "holy", that is belonging completely to God, and we define ourselves as "sinners", that is people who are far from God and even opposed to Him. In our prayer, although we go beyond the actual words of Elizabeth, the request that we make to Mary to intercede for us before God, who has chosen her and brought her into such close union with Himself, corresponds perfectly to the reality. With the "Hail Mary" we go back to the beginning, taking up the most original understanding of Mary and expressing the most authentic attitude towards her.

The enthusiasm of Elizabeth

Until now we have been concentrating on the content of Elizabeth's words. The evangelist puts the

76   *Mary the Mother of the Lord in the New Testament*

words in context (1,41-42). Elizabeth hears Mary's greeting and she feels the child in her womb leap for joy. She is filled with the Holy Spirit and cries out in a loud voice.

Because of the presence of the Holy Spirit in her, Elizabeth is able to recognise what God has brought about in Mary, and this does not leave her cold or indifferent, but touches and moves her deeply. She can no longer keep within herself what she has come to recognise but she has to express it with a loud cry. Elizabeth is the first human being who recognises Mary as the mother of the Lord. The meeting of Mary and Elizabeth tells us something about our relationship with God. With our normal human powers we are not capable of recognising the dignity and position of Mary, and therefore we need the Holy Spirit. The ability to recognise God's work is a gift of the Spirit. The one who is able to recognise who Mary is, cannot remain unfeeling and dumb, as if nothing had taken place. The gift of recognition makes a deep impression within and leads to enthusiasm and a desire to communicate the marvellous things that one has discovered.

If we remain cold in relation to Mary and are not able to understand what is so important about her, we are lacking in the Spirit, and need to pray for this gift. Only the Holy Spirit gives us the possibility to understand the action of God. What God has done in Mary is truly good news. God chose her and blessed her, and through her son, gives the fullness of life to all.

c) Mary is blessed and full of faith

Elizabeth is the first person who recognises what God has done in Mary and she also understands how Mary has reacted to God's approach. Elizabeth says: *"Blessed is she who has believed in the fulfilment of the words of the Lord "* (1.45). Characteristic of Mary is her faith, by which she accepts what God says to her as completely dependable. For this reason Mary is blessed and overflows with joy.

The faith of Mary

In this scene we come to understand more about the proper human response to God, who makes known His plan. At first is the word, which precedes the event itself, and this word announces and promises something. The fact itself is not yet present. The one who believes does not have to wait until the event takes place, until she can see it with her own eyes and touch it with her own hands, but she puts her trust in the word of God. The believer recognises that the word of God is completely consistent and supremely trustworthy, because behind it stands the power of God who cannot lie, and who will accomplish His plan. Faith goes beyond the present and what occurs in it; faith introduces into the present what God will bring about in the future.

The blessedness that Elizabeth refers to her cousin, presupposes that the word of God has been addressed to Mary. This is mentioned in the preceding scene in which the messenger of God says to Mary: *"Behold, you will conceive and bear a son.... He will be great and will be called Son of the Most High* " (1,31-32), and goes on, "*The Holy Spirit will descend upon you and the power of the Most High will cover you with its shadow. He who is to be born will therefore be Holy and will be called Son of God.......Nothing is impossible for God* " (1,35-37). All of these words refer to what God will bring about in the future through Mary. She trusts in God, accepts His word as true and complies with what He is asking of her. Faith offers Mary access to the plan and to the word of God and binds her ever more closely to Him. The divine creative power works within Mary who believes and who entrusts herself to the word of God, and so she becomes the mother of the Lord. Mary has to continue to have such faith until God accomplishes all that has been announced.

The Risen Lord reproaches the two disciples on the road to Emmaus: "*Foolish and slow of heart to believe the word of the prophets!* " (Lk 24,25). Mary is neither foolish nor slow to believe, but she is wise and alert. She is a model of faith for us who are on this journey through life and directed towards the future. The word of God moves us to believe that God is showing us the right path in Jesus, and that our destiny is safe in God's hands, as we are led safely to the goal of human life. We cannot verify any of this but it is communicated to us in the message of Jesus and we must simply believe in the word of God. Our Creator does not treat us like puppets; we have been allowed to penetrate what is happening to us and what is our destiny. God points out to us the way and what is our future by means of the word that is addressed to us. If we accept this word in faith, we open ourselves in full awareness to what God will accomplish within us.

The blessedness of Mary

The angel introduced his message to Mary with an invitation: *"Rejoice. God has filled you with grace. The Lord is with you "* (1,28). Elizabeth ends her words by saying: *"Blessed is she who has believed in the fulfilment of the words of the Lord"* (1,45). Both cases have to do with joy, founded on the action of God. Blessedness means pure joy that penetrates everything, fills and overflows. By calling Mary "blessed", Elizabeth says to her that she has every reason to be joyful. The foundation of this joy is her faith in the fulfilment of the word of God. This joy will break forth later in Mary when she proclaims her song of praise, the *Magnificat*.

In the *Magnificat*, she declares: *"Behold, from now on all generations will call me blessed, because the Almighty has done great things in me "* (1,48). Mary speaks to Elizabeth and affirms that the praise that the latter has offered (*"blessed is she "*) will be taken up by all generations. In all ages Mary will be admired and she will be recognised as having every reason to be overflowing with joy. Mary's faith is not mentioned here but the unique work of God is explicitly made the foundation of all this. With creative power God has made Mary the mother of His Son. In our days when we call Mary "blessed", we unite ourselves with all those people throughout the ages starting with Elizabeth, who have praised the work of God in the mother of the Lord, as she herself prophesied in the Gospel.

The blessing expressed by a woman in the crowd: *"Blessed the womb that bore you and the breasts that gave you milk "*, is explained and amplified by Jesus: *"Blessed rather are those who hear the word of God and obey it "* (Lk 11,27-28). Jesus is not casting doubts on his mother's blessedness, but is making it dependent upon her relationship with God and with His word. Mary entrusted herself completely to the word of God and in this way is a model for us.

Characteristic of Mary are her faith and her blessedness. She welcomes with open arms the word of God and is completely available to God's work in her. This is the foundation for an unlimited joy.

3. MARY PRAISES THE GREATNESS OF GOD (1,46-55)

After Elizabeth has expressed what she has been given to understand about the great events (1,41-45), Mary begins to speak. She speaks exclusively of God and her words reveal a profound knowledge of the Lord. Through her song of praise we can see God with her eyes. Mary proclaims above all her own experience of God (1,46-49), and sees this against the background of how God normally acts in relation to human beings (1,50-53) and especially how God treats His own people, Israel (1,54-55).

a) Mary praises God (1,46-49)

God has come down to Mary and has acted in her in a very powerful way. Mary becomes ever more aware of how good God is and what wonders He has worked in her. She overflows with joy and she praises the mercy and faithfulness of God.

Mary's joy

The first word of the angel to Mary is: *"Rejoice "* (1,28), and Elizabeth concludes her little speech by saying, *"Blessed is she who has believed" (1,45)*. It is clear in both cases that Mary has every reason to be joyful but until this moment, she is depicted as reflecting and meditating and the evangelist has not mentioned any manifestation of joy. Elizabeth's enthusiasm is the final spur to Mary's explosion of joy.

Mary's canticle of praise is the fruit of a profound experience that is profoundly understood. Her soul and spirit, that is her whole being, are focused on God. Mary has experienced in her own self the stupendous action of God and now praises Him. Her happiness and her joy are so great that they overflow from her and are communicated aloud with exultation. Mary is full to overflowing with joy.

The action of God

Mary recognises the Lord as her saviour, *"because he has looked upon the lowliness of his servant "*. She is fully aware of what has happened. Before God she is an insignificant creature, one of many. Before the world, she is an insignificant young girl from an unknown country village of Nazareth. She holds no important position and no one need take account of her.

From the human point of view, she does not count. However God has looked upon her, not like one who looks down on others from a position of superiority despising the little ones, but with a look of love and predilection. God has lifted her up from her position of insignificance and has become her saviour. Every act of love on the part of God is a saving action, because He leads people to Himself, and in this way brings about their salvation.

When Mary responded to the message of the angel, she called herself, "*the servant of the Lord*" (1,38), and so also in this occasion. Hers is a humble but at the same time joyful recognition of the reality. She recognises that she is bound to the service that God has entrusted to her, and she is also aware that there is no greater honour or more wonderful task than being able to serve God. The words of the angel: "*You have found favour with God*" (1,30), and the service for which Mary has been chosen have conquered her heart. She has understood the changes that the action of God has produced in her human situation. Her spirit and her soul join together in one song of joy.

The praise of all generations

God brought Mary out of her insignificant position. A sign and consequence is that she will be called blessed by all generations. It is possible for a person to attract attention to herself during her life. After death, most people are forgotten sooner or later. There remains no memory of them and it is as if they never existed.

Chapter III: Mary in the Gospel of Luke

Mary's affirmation is contrasted to this common destiny: *"All generations will call me blessed"* (1,48). There is no generation that will forget her or fail to mention her. In all ages, not only will she be remembered but she will also be called "blessed". She will attract the attention of all generations who will look upon her with wonder and exultation.

The foundation of all of this is not Mary considered in herself but as the one who has welcomed the divine action in her life. Mary herself underlines this: *"All generations will call me blessed because the Almighty has done great things in me"* (1,48-49). Here Mary calls God *"the Almighty"*, referring in particular to the divine power, which the angel reminds her, has no limits (1,37). Mary becomes the mother of God's Son by the power of the Almighty (1,35). This fact will be remembered by all generations and will make up the principal content of her blessedness, which is hers by virtue of being the mother of the Lord. The way in which she has become mother, that is by a virginal conception, attracts the attention of all. It is to the virgin mother that the blessing of all generations is directed.

Mary's canticle of praise speaks of God, and precisely of what God has done in her. Here we can note a fundamental difference between the *Magnificat* and Zechariah's canticle of praise (the *Benedictus*). In the latter, Zechariah speaks of the coming of the Messiah and his precursor but he himself has no importance (1,68-79), while in the *Magnificat*, Mary does not mention the Messiah, but turns the attention to God and to herself. Clearly her great task is that of becoming the mother of the Messiah by the power of God but she is not an irrelevant instrument in the hands of God, who looks upon her, which is the foundation for all generations to call her blessed.

b) Mary and God Most Holy

Mary goes beyond what she herself has experienced and she describes how God generally treats human beings. She brings to mind certain human behaviours and indicates how God looks on these. In this way it becomes clear the way in which God evaluates human actions. Above all we have the affirmation: *"Holy is His name"* (1,49). In the Scriptures what distinguishes God from all creatures is holiness. The seraphim who stand before God's throne call out three times this divine attribute (Is 6,3; cf. Apoc 4,8). In this way the Scriptures express that God is incomparably superior to all things and is completely unique. Therefore there is but one God. Nothing can equal God or compete with Him and nothing can stand before His face. The Lord is God, from whom everything depends. This all-powerful and most holy God decided to do a wonderful work in Mary. God's holiness determines the way in which He acts in relation to human beings.

Mercy for those who respect God

Mary affirms: *"From generation to generation His mercy is shown to those who fear Him"* (1,50). This does not mean people who are afraid of God but those who respect Him, show veneration and recognise Him as their God and Lord. They confess that God is their Creator and recognise that they have received everything from Him and that it is right to listen to His word and do His will. These people in every age can count on the mercy of God, who will not treat them with harshness or be distant from them. When they are in need, they will experience the divine goodness, understanding and assistance.

The judgement that God makes

God does not necessarily respect the relationships and the systems established by human beings and the attitudes that determine our life. God will somehow correct these unless they follow the divine will. Mary brings to mind some essential attitudes that regulate the relationship with God, with other human beings, with the goods of the earth, and she shows how these are judged by God.

She speaks of those whose hearts are full of pride, of the arrogant and the presumptuous. Their behaviour is the opposite of those who respect God. They do not recognise God as their Lord but they want to govern themselves. Assuming a total independence and freedom, they are guided by the following criteria: "I will make the final decision about my life. I will do what I want and what pleases me. I do not need to listen to anyone else or to be instructed by anyone else. I will not follow the counsel of anybody. I want to be master of my own life". The one who builds his or her life on these principles cannot stand before God. The proud live according to their own arrogance and they have forgotten that they did not bring themselves into existence, and so they can never have complete control over their own lives. Their Creator and Lord will bring them face to face with reality.

Mary then affirms: *"He has overthrown the powerful ones from their thrones and He has raised up the humble"* (1,52). Jesus himself gave this definition of the powerful ones: *"The kings of the nations rule them and those who have power call themselves benefactors"*, and then he goes on: *"For you, it must not be so; but the one who is greatest among you must become the smallest and the one who rules like one who serves"* (Lk 22,25-26). The powerful ones are those who possess power and on whom others depend. They do not use their power to do good to others and to serve them but for their own advantage. They make others experience their dependence on them and they benefit from their own power. They want to be honoured and recognised as people with power. People like this are not only found in the upper echelons of society, but at all levels. Whoever treats his or her neighbour with this kind of attitude cannot be pleasing to God. Mary affirms that God will put an end to behaviour like this, even though she does not specify when or how. On the other hand, God raises up the lowly. A significant example of this is what God has done in Mary herself (cf. 1,48). She was never proclaimed queen in Jerusalem but she shared in the fate of her son until she was assumed into heaven.

Finally Mary declares: *"He has filled the hungry with good things and sent the rich away with empty hands* " (1,53). The rich have at their disposition an abundance of earthly goods (cf. Lk 12,16-21). Like the rich man in the parable of Jesus who ignored Lazarus at his gate, they use their goods to live in opulence and give themselves over to all kinds of pleasures. Those who are hungry on the other hand do not have even the possibility of getting the necessities for life. Jesus says to the rich: " *Woe to you, who are rich, because you have already received your consolation* " (Lk 6,24). God will not leave this situation forever. Those who are totally attached to the good things of the earth and who live to use them at their pleasure, are sent away by God empty handed. In their hearts there is no room for God or for His word. The poor are waiting for God and open to receive all God's gifts.

Mary brings us before the Holy God. Only those who treat God with respect and orientate their lives according to God's will can be pleasing to Him.

c) Mary and Abraham (1,54-55)

At the end of her canticle of praise, Mary speaks of the action of God in relation to the people of Israel: "*He has helped Israel, His servant, remembering His mercy, as He had promised to our fathers, Abraham and his descendants, for ever* " (1,54-55). The people of Israel have a special relationship with God, who chose them and called them to be His servant (cf. Is 41,8). God cared for this people, making sure of their survival. God is bound to this attitude because of His mercy and the promise made to Abraham and his descendants. The divine mercy is for all who respect God (1,50) but is particularly addressed to the people of Israel. In the promise made to Abraham, God is expressly bound to take care of him and his descendants.

The fulfilment of the promise

The great things that the Almighty has done in Mary are part of God's care for the people of Israel and are an expression of the divine mercy. These things bring to a fulfilment the promises made to Israel. Abraham is the patriarch of the people of Israel, and with his election the history of this people begins. When he was chosen, God made him this promise: "*I will make you a great people and I will bless you. I will make your name great and you will become a blessing. I will bless those who bless you, and those that curse you, I will curse. All the families of the earth will be blessed in you.*" (Gen 12,2-3; cf. 22,15-18). Through Abraham God blesses, conserves and promotes life.

This action of God reaches its culmination in Mary. Elizabeth affirms: "*Blessed are you among women and blessed is the fruit of your womb* " (1,42). Through Mary, God gives the people of Israel its last and definitive king. The son of Mary "*will reign for ever over the house of Jacob and his kingdom will have no end* " (1,33). He is the king through whom God is involved in the life of the people and takes care of them. Through this king, the promise of blessing made by God is brought to fulfilment in the most complete and unsurpassable way. "Blessing" means life. Jesus overcomes death at the resurrection and enters into immortal, eternal life with God. As king of his people, he leads those who trust in him to the same end. Those who are faithful to him will share together with him in the fullness of eternal life.

Abraham is the head of his people inasmuch as regards natural earthly life. Through Mary God gives the Son, who leads to the fullness of life. This life is not transmitted by means of normal procreation, but is shared with those who believe in Jesus and follow him. Mary and her son have become an even greater blessing than Abraham, because through them God transmits eternal life.

Acceptance in faith

The word in which God expresses the promise must be received properly by people. When God promises Abraham a son, the Scriptures tell us: *"He believed in the Lord, and this was credited to him as justice "* (Gen 15,6). St. Paul in particular stresses that the decisive action of Abraham was his faith. He writes of this in the whole of chapter four of the letter to the Romans: *"By God's promise, he (Abraham) did not hesitate in unbelief, but he grew strong in faith and gave glory to God, fully convinced that God was capable of bringing to fulfilment whatever had been promised. For this reason it was reckoned to him as righteousness "* (Rom 4,20-22). The Apostle sees in the reaction of Abraham a great example of what faith means and therefore sees in him "the father of all of us" before God, because of his faith.

Elizabeth says to Mary: *"Blessed is she who believed in the fulfilment of the words of the Lord"* (1,45). She also recognises that Mary's faith is decisive. What Paul says about Abraham, one could also say about Mary. She did not doubt what had been communicated to her by the angel. She gave glory to God and she was fully convinced that God has the power to accomplish what had been announced to her. Mary is an exemplary daughter of Abraham.

The old covenant, the history of God's dealings with the people of Israel, begins with the call of Abraham to whom God promises a blessing and who accepts the word of God with faith. The new covenant, which is God's definitive work of salvation, begins with the call of Mary. She also believes in the word of God that is directed to her. Mary is blessed above all, because she became a mother by means of the creative power of God, and gave birth to the one through whom God gives not just an earthly existence but eternal life.

Israel is called "the servant of the Lord". Choosing Mary as a servant and making her the mother of His Son, God brings to fulfilment the blessing promised to Israel. The people were often unfaithful to their election and to their service of God, showing themselves to be an untrustworthy servant. Mary takes the place of the servant. She is the perfect servant who believes in the word of the Lord and who is totally available for service. She is a model of faith and of willingness to serve. In the same way that St. Paul considers Abraham to be "the father of us all" because of his exemplary faith, so also we could consider Mary

Chapter III: Mary in the Gospel of Luke 91

"the mother of us all" because of her faith. At the beginning of the old covenant, there is Abraham as father in faith; at the beginning of the new covenant there is Mary as mother in faith. Both are chosen and blessed by God in different ways.

4. MARY AT BETHLEHEM (2,1-20)

In one of the most well known passages of his Gospel, Luke tells us about the birth of Jesus and the announcement to the shepherds. Here we limit ourselves to what he tells us about Mary.

The birth of Jesus

The evangelist recounts the birth of Jesus with few and simple words. However he describes in a rather detailed way the reason why Jesus was born in Bethlehem. Like all citizens of the Roman empire, Mary and Joseph were subject to the rule of Caesar Augustus. By his decree, they had to go to Bethlehem to register. Because of the influence of Roman authority, Jesus was born where king David came from. Roman authority will exercise even greater influence over his death. Jesus will die on the cross, condemned to this death by Pontius Pilate, governor of Judea in the reign of the Emperor Tiberius.

For the second time in a brief period, Mary made the long journey from Nazareth to Judea. Totally taken up with her great vocation and the great mystery of her life, she went in haste to her cousin Elizabeth (1,39).

She was confirmed in her faith and, in her great joy, she gave homage to God in her canticle of exulting praise. Now as a young expectant mother she makes the same journey along with Joseph.

Just as she is subject to the power of the state, so too she is subject to the laws of nature. She is not the one who chooses the time or the place of her son's birth. She has to adapt to the ordinary circumstances of life and she seeks always what is best. When the time comes for her to give birth, she produces a son. The evangelist stresses that this is "her" son and that he is the "first born". With regard to Elizabeth, Luke recounted the circumstances in much less detail: "*She gave birth to a son*" (1,57). Mary is already aware of the position and the mission of her son (1,31-33), and this is confirmed very shortly (2,11.17). He is her son in a very special way and is the "*fruit of her womb*" (1,42). The fact that he is named as the first born does not mean that Mary had other children after him, but that he is consecrated in a very special way to God, and it refers to the later event of the presentation in the Temple (2,22-23). The dignity and the greatness of Mary consist in being the mother of this child, who belongs in a very special way to God.

After giving birth to a son, Mary wraps him in swaddling clothes. It seems that no one helped her at the birth. She has in her arms a little, defenceless child, who, like any new born, needs love and care. Until now he has been protected in his mother's womb and received directly from her everything he needed for life. Now his mother wraps him in swaddling clothes, which keep him warm and sustain him. This is her first act of care and

Chapter III: Mary in the Gospel of Luke

love for her child. She will continue to pour out her love on him and take care of him in every way as he grows and develops. The child's being wrapped in swaddling clothes is a symbol of his dependence and inability to take care of himself. It shows that his mother welcomed him and cared for him efficiently. Even after the birth, mother and child remain closely united.

Mary wrapped her newborn child and placed him in a manger, meant for animals. From this it can be deduced that she gave birth in a stall, near to the animals. She could find no better place and she can only offer her little son a rough substitute for a cradle. In this way was born the Son of the Most High. This situation shows the great task that Mary had accepted. She finds herself in poor surroundings and she adapts. She does everything possible for her child in a situation of absolute poverty and need. She shows herself to be a woman who acts realistically. She does not daydream about better or ideal circumstances but she does everything possible for her child in the situation in which she finds herself. Everything in the story of Jesus' birth is shorn of external splendour; the extraordinary event takes place in such a poor and ordinary way. In this way Mary fulfils her service for the people of God and gives birth to the Son of God (1,32-35), the Saviour, the Christ and the Lord (2,11).

Mary meditated on all these things

The shepherds, who had learned from the messengers sent by God what had happened there in the stall beside the animals, went to find Mary, Joseph and the baby, who lay in the manger (2,16). They told what they had heard. At this point Luke tells us: *"Mary kept in her heart all that had happened and continued to meditate on it"* (2,19). Mary could not grasp the full import of everything that had happened immediately but she stored up everything in her heart. With patience and love she took care of everything that Jesus needed. We imitate her in the rosary, by means of which we ponder on the path taken by Jesus and his meaning for us personally and for the life of the world.

The meditation of Mary is characterised above all by two elements. She ponders on her own experience and on the word of God. Mary is subject to the normal ways of the world and she gives birth in very poor circumstances. Through the word of God she comes to know what is the position and the task of her son. Neither of these elements, her own experience or the word of God, can be neglected or diminished. They complete each other and together form a whole. However the way in which they go together cannot be understood totally from the outset, and so Mary must seek to gradually grasp the whole picture by a patient pondering. Mary does not waste anything but ponders and believes. She accepts the difficulty and the incomprehensibility of her situation but goes beyond it, and entrusts herself to the word of God. Her son is a defenceless little baby, born in a stall, and at the same time is the Son of God and the Saviour of the world.

Bethlehem shows us two essential characteristics of Mary. She acts according to the circumstances but she

Chapter III: Mary in the Gospel of Luke

is not blindly absorbed by activity. She ponders with patience and with faith; she entrusts herself to the word of God and seeks to understand everything she sees and experiences in its light.

5. MARY WITH HER CHILD IN THE TEMPLE (2,22-40)

Jesus is circumcised and is given his name at Bethlehem, where he was born (2,21). Forty days after his birth he was taken to Jerusalem, to the Temple, where two prophetic figures, Simeon and Anna, speak of salvation and of Jesus as the Messiah (2,22-38). Then Mary and Joseph take the baby to Nazareth, where he grows up and spends the greater part of his life (2,39-40). Throughout all of this Mary shows herself to be "the servant of the Lord" (1,38). She fulfils perfectly the will of God, revealed through the Law of Moses (2,22-24.39), and experiences how the position and destiny of her son profoundly and sorrowfully influence her own life (2,34-35). Mary does not lead an independent and autonomous existence, following her own plans, but her whole life is determined by her union with God and by the intimate connection with her son.

To the Temple in Jerusalem

In conformity with the Law of the Lord (cf. Lev 12,3), Jesus is circumcised on the 8th day after his birth and in this way enters into the covenant that God made with Abraham. The child receives the name that was communicated by the angel and that God had decreed for him (1,31). Everything is done in perfect obedience to the will of God; nothing is left to human arbitrariness.

Then forty days after his birth, Jesus was taken to the Temple in Jerusalem. This was the day set aside for a woman who had given birth to offer sacrifice for her purification (cf. Lv 12,1-8). For this sacrifice a lamb and a dove were required. Mary offers a pair of doves, which was a concession to the poor. This situation shows that Mary followed the normal path and despite her modest circumstances, she completely fulfilled the Law that God had given to the people.

Being the first born (2,7), Jesus belongs to God in a special way according to the Law (Ex 13,2.12-15). This prescription of the Law was intended to stress that everything belongs to the Creator, from whom everything comes. Returning to God by means of a sacrifice something that had first been received from God, people recognised this fundamental reality. The Law prescribed that the first born of animals had to be offered in sacrifice, while children were to be redeemed with money.

Luke does not say that Jesus was redeemed but that he was presented and consecrated to the Lord. Jesus belongs to God in a very particular way as he owed his earthly existence to a unique act of God's creative power. At the Annunciation, the messenger of God had already affirmed this: *"He who will be born will therefore be holy, and will be called Son of God"* (1,35). The one who is holy, that is who belongs totally to God, and who is God's Son, is now brought to the Temple, which is the place of God's presence in the midst of the people. So, for the first time Jesus enters his Father's house.

For Mary it must have been a cause of great joy to bring the Son of God into God's house, as well as a step forward in the journey of her own vocation. Mary brings to God he whom she conceived and bore through the power of God. Her joy is accompanied by the awareness that her son does not belong to her, but is completely subject to the will of God. Mary will only discover gradually what this reality will involve.

The words of Simeon

When Mary and Joseph took the baby into the Temple to do what the Law prescribed, Simeon took Jesus in his arms. He welcomes the child almost like a man of God into God's own house. However he also welcomes Jesus as the great gift given him by God in his old age. At the Annunciation, the angel spoke of Jesus as the Son of the Most High, as the one who would reign forever over the house of Jacob (1,32-33), and to the shepherds as the Saviour, the Messiah and the Lord (2,11). Simeon looks beyond the people of Israel and he recognises that Jesus is destined by God to be the salvation of all people, the light to the pagans and the glory of the people of Israel (2,30-32).

Until this moment there have only been great things said of Jesus. The poor circumstances of his coming into the world perhaps gave pause for thought and diluted the joy. With his final words Simeon throws a dark shadow over the future of Jesus and also of Mary: "*He is here for the ruin and for the rising of many in Israel, a sign of contradiction so that the thoughts of many hearts will be revealed. And a sword will pierce your soul*" (2,34-35). Simeon declares Jesus' destiny from God and correspondingly what will happen to Mary.

The coming of Jesus has contradictory effects among people. Some fall to their ruin, while others rise up because of him. He is not a Messiah who is exalted by everyone but he meets strong resistance. However nothing is said at this point that such hostility will lead him to a violent death.

Mary participates in Jesus' destiny in the depths of her soul, that is with her whole being. She gave birth to him, protected and guarded his life as a child. The life of Jesus is her life. The sword is the weapon that hurts and kills; by its very nature it is hostile to life. What will happen to Jesus, the hostility that he will experience, pierces Mary and strikes her to the core of her being, just like a sword cuts and pierces. Mary is united with Jesus completely and so what hurts him hurts her. His destiny is her destiny. As the mother of the Messiah, she experiences not only a great joy (1,28), but also great grief.

In all of this, Mary is the model for every disciple of Jesus. The disciple must not be in a cold and distant relationship with the Master, but must open his or her life in all its aspects to the destiny of Jesus.

With this awareness, Mary returns to Nazareth and spends with her son the first twelve years of his life. These are the years in which the child depends to a great extent on the care of the mother and when she is absorbed by the needs of the child. These are years of the greatest communion between mother and child. However this child does not belong to Mary, but to God and to the task that has been given to him. This will strike and pierce Mary like a sword.

6. Mary and Jesus at twelve years of age

Luke tells us that Jesus went up three times to Jerusalem: the first time as a baby (2,21), then as a twelve year old child and finally when he went there as an adult to fulfil his destiny (9,51). An Israelite at twelve years of age was bound to observe the Law. He was no longer considered to be a child but a young adult, just as responsible as any member of the people of God. At the Passover feast, the people remembered with joy and gratitude the great work of God, who had rescued Israel from the slavery of Egypt and made them His people. Jesus would bring his task to completion within the feast. Through his death and resurrection, he set free not only Israel but humanity in its entirety, from its subjection to sin and death. He reconciled all people with God and opened the way towards the fullness of life. This is the way that God established for the salvation of all.

In search of Jesus

When Mary participated in the feast of Passover, she no longer led her son by the hand like a child. She

100   *Mary the Mother of the Lord in the New Testament*

gave him freedom so that he could have some independence. This explains the fact that Mary and Joseph only became aware of Jesus' absence on the evening of the first day of the return journey. They had not checked that he had started out on the journey home from Jerusalem together with all the other pilgrims. They were profoundly concerned at his absence and they began to search for him until they had found him. They are convinced that Jesus was entrusted to their care and that they are responsible for him. Their concern and the love they have for Jesus makes them take every care and to keep on searching for him.

In dialogue with Jesus

When they find him, Mary asks Jesus a question, and this is the last thing that Mary says in Luke's Gospel. Jesus responds with two of his own questions. These are his first words as reported by Luke. In this unique dialogue the questions of mother and son are set off against each other.

Mary says to Jesus: "*My child, why have you done this to us? Your father and I were looking for you and we were very worried* " (2,48). The term "my child" expresses the intimate relationship between Mary and Jesus. In this question is concentrated all the wonder and the pain at the behaviour of Jesus. Why had he not said that he wanted to stay in Jerusalem? Why had he forced them to make a long journey and a frantic search? Is this not inconsiderate and disrespectful from

Chapter III: Mary in the Gospel of Luke 101

a twelve year old who is not yet mature enough to be aware of the consequences of his behaviour? By her question Mary asks Jesus to clarify his behaviour and to explain his reasons.

Jesus answers with two questions of his own: *"Why were you looking for me? Did you not know that I must be busy about my Father's affairs?"* (2,49) Just as his parents wondered why Jesus, without saying anything, remained in Jerusalem, forcing them to search anxiously for him, so also he seems to be surprised because they were looking for him and that they did not let him go home to them when he decided.

Jesus refers to God as his Father and he reminds Mary and Joseph what the purpose of his life is: he must be busy about his Father's affairs. The relationship with his Father is above all others, and in the light of this, even his relationship with his mother is secondary. Jesus knows that he is bound in an unconditional manner to God and therefore it is of first importance to him what has to do with God. He is guided by the Father and seeks always to fulfil the will of God. Therefore he remained in the Father's house, to which he had been taken as a baby to be presented and consecrated to God. He remained behind to discuss the word of the Father with the doctors of Israel. Jesus let himself be guided by listening to the will of God, not only in this present situation, but also throughout the whole of his life. He always followed the will of the Father, fulfilling the task that had been given to him, even though this provoked astonishment in his Mother.

Jesus does not attempt to justify himself nor does he give a detailed explanation but he does make it clear that he did not act on a whim or in an inconsiderate manner. He states the foundation of his whole life: God the Father and His will. In a brief but difficult way, Mary learns what is implied in having to let her son be free so that he might bind himself unconditionally to his Father.

Mary's reaction

Luke says of Mary and Joseph that *"they did not understand his words"* (2,50). They cannot see the link between the behaviour and the words of Jesus. Without giving them any further explanation, Jesus returns with them to Nazareth and lives in obedience to them.

The evangelist describes Mary's reaction like this: *"His mother kept in her heart everything that happened to her"* (2,51). Luke had already referred to Mary's reaction to events after the birth of Jesus when the shepherds came to pay their homage (2,19). Mary does not ask for any further explanation and has no word of reproof. She keeps in her heart what she has experienced and believes the word of her twelve year old son, according to which he must be busy about his Father's affairs. Even though she does not know the details of God's plan or of Jesus' future, she entrusts herself to the guidance of God and remains bound to her son with all her heart. She tries to see and to understand but she is patient; she knows how to wait and how to live with an incomplete understanding. She does not make her relationship with God and her son depend on her level of understanding. Her behaviour is profoundly rooted and therefore can sustain her. What characterises her is her trust in the guidance of God with an unconditional faith and her indissoluble communion of life with her son.

In these circumstances too Mary is the model for every disciple of Jesus. Many of our questions will not receive an answer and we will not be given a complete understanding of all things. Precisely for this reason we are called to an unconditional faith in God and an indissoluble communion of life with Jesus. Our faith in God the Father and our relationship with His Son Jesus must always be greater than our understanding.

7. MARY AND THE PUBLIC LIFE OF JESUS

In the first two chapters of Luke's Gospel, Jesus is only spoken of where Mary is present. In these chapters we find a rich and vivid image of her. In the following twenty two chapters of the Gospel, this situation changes. These chapters refer to the work of Jesus right through to his resurrection and Mary all but disappears. This does not mean that she had no part to play in her son's activities. Simeon had predicted the time that Jesus would become a sign of contradiction (2,34). He also announced that Mary would receive a grievous blow; a sword would pierce her very soul (2,35). Mary no longer lives side by side with her son but she remains close to him spiritually and is full of concern for him.

The evangelist refers to instances where mother and son were near each other. When Jesus came to Nazareth and was rejected, this must have caused a profound disturbance for his Mother (4,16-30). During his ministry, his mother and his brothers go looking for him, but it seems that he does not receive them. (8,19-21). A woman in the crowd is so impressed by everything that Jesus does that she declares his mother blessed (11,27-28). We will now look at how these passages complete the picture of Mary.

The activity of Jesus in Nazareth (4,16-30)

Luke strongly underlines the connection of Jesus with Nazareth. After the episode in the Temple when Jesus was twelve years of age, the evangelist tells us: *"He returned with them to Nazareth and lived in obedience to them"* (2,51). Jesus spent the greater part of his life inserted into the community of Nazareth and in the family of Joseph and Mary. The life in this little village was his world.

When he recounts the visit of Jesus to Nazareth, Luke tells us: *"He went back to Nazareth, where he had grown up, and he entered the synagogue on the sabbath day as was his custom and he got up to read the Scriptures "* (4,16). The evangelist tells us explicitly that Jesus grew up in Nazareth and also that he went every sabbath into the synagogue. He stresses the very close bond that Jesus had with Nazareth and with the celebration of the sabbath there. One can presume that Luke does not intend to say Jesus arrived in Nazareth and went straight to the synagogue, but that he went to his Mother's house and from there on the sabbath, went to the synagogue.

In the story of the disagreement between the people of Nazareth and Jesus, Mary does not appear. They ask: *"Is he not the son of Joseph?"* (4,22; in a different form in Mt 13,55 and Mk 6,3). However the scene takes place in Nazareth where Mary lives and where Jesus grew up. Here Jesus appears as a sign of contradiction, so much so that his fellow citizens of Nazareth want to throw him off a precipice (4,30). Here the words of Simeon come true about a sword piercing Mary's soul (2,35). Even though Luke does not say so explicitly, from the context one can discern a characteristic of his gospel as being that from the very beginning of Jesus' public ministry, Mary feels in her own heart the fact that people reject Jesus because of her closeness to him. From the very beginning her soul is grievously wounded.

The visit of Jesus' relatives (8,19-21)

In Luke's Gospel, the coming of the Mother and brothers of Jesus is linked immediately to the discourse of Jesus to a large crowd (8,4-18). The theme of this discourse is "right listening"(7 times) and the "word of God" (4 times). When Jesus has explained the parable, he states: *"The seed that falls on good earth are those who, after having heard the word with a good and perfect heart, guard it and produce fruit by their perseverance"* (8,15).

Jesus takes up this theme again in his reaction to the arrival of his relatives: *"My mother and my brothers are those who listen to the word of God and put it into practice "* (8,21). Everything that has gone before is concluded and confirmed.

Some people think that with these words Jesus wanted to distance himself from his relatives and so what he is really saying is: Unlike blood relatives, those who are members of Jesus' real family are those who hear the word of God and who put it into practice. Others hold the opposite opinion and believe that Jesus is referring to his relatives as models of right listening and doing. Therefore what these people believe the text means is: My mother and my brothers are those who hear the word of God and who put it into practice. Both of these interpretations seem to be unilateral. It is certain that Jesus wants to stress listening to the word of God that actually has effects on daily life, and he says that this is decisive in whether or not one has a relationship with him. This is the rule for everyone including his own blood family.

With regard to Mary, we should not forget that her way of reacting to the word of God has already been declared blessed: *"Blessed is she who believed in the fulfilment of the words of the Lord "* (1,45). Her fundamental attitude is to entrust herself to the word of God and follow it. Mary is not bound to Jesus only by virtue of her being his mother, but also by means of her reception, full of faith and obedience, of the word of God. Precisely because she believed in the word of God, she became the Mother of God's Son.

The blessedness of the Mother of Jesus (11,27-28)

In a later phase of Jesus' activity, the evangelist says: *"While he was saying this, a woman in the crowd raised her voice and said: 'Blessed is the womb that bore you and that breasts that you suckled'. But he said: 'Blessed rather are those who hear the word of God and put it into practice!'"* (11,27-28).

The woman who speaks here is profoundly impressed by Jesus. Her admiration for him makes her declare that his mother is blessed. What happiness must the mother of such a son have! How authentic and spontaneous are the feelings of this woman can be seen from the fact that she interrupts Jesus in the middle of a discourse to express her admiration. The words of Jesus strike her and, more precisely his power against the demons, which is described in the preceding passage (11,14-26).

In her words of blessing, the woman brings to mind the close and reciprocal relationship between mother and son and the meaning they have for each other. She says clearly how much a son owes to his mother. The womb of the mother surrounds, protects and nourishes the child before its birth; the mother's breasts give nourishment long after the birth. The child receives life from its mother but the happiness of the mother depends a great deal on the condition of her child. The words of the woman in the crowd express this clearly: the powerful actions of Jesus must make his mother very happy.

Jesus also expresses this very close relationship between mother and son during his *via crucis*, when he speaks to the weeping women. They are weeping because of what is happening to him, which is his destiny (23,27). To them Jesus foretells the times when it will be said: *"Blessed are the barren, the wombs that have not borne children and the breasts that have not suckled "*(23,29; cf. 21,23). Here Jesus proclaims blessed those who do not have children. The reason is that they will not have to witness what their children must suffer in the anguish of the future times. Here also the profound bond between mother and child is expressed, and how she is affected by the destiny, good or bad, of her children. The child owes its life to its mother. The life of the child is always in some way the life of the mother, whether in joy or in sorrow. Simeon announced this to Mary and he considered her life to be a reflection of the destiny of Jesus (2,34-35). Often in Luke's Gospel there is a reference to how a mother and child affect each other's life. Mary and Jesus are included in this.

In his answer, Jesus does not reject the blessing of the woman but he enlarges upon it and completes it. He takes up what has caused the woman's marvel. She admires him for his words and actions that are full of power. Her words of blessing only refer to the mother of such a son. The blessing stated by Jesus has no limits; it is directed towards all those who receive his message as the word of God. He declares blessed not only his own mother, but all those who receive and put into practice his words. Through his words, Jesus shows to everyone the way towards the fullness of life and blessing. All people can count themselves fortunate because they are able to listen to him and through him know the will of God (cf. 10,23). Jesus is not important only for his own mother but for every human being. Here can also be seen the awareness of Jesus, who understands the universal significance of his own mission.

Jesus does not exclude Mary from his words of blessing. She is the one who is open to the word of God. For this reason Elizabeth has already declared her blessed and so she receives the first blessing in Luke's Gospel (1,45). The blessing pronounced by the woman in the crowd is for the mother of such a son with such a great mission. Mary is bound to her son as mother but also as hearer of his word. Through Jesus, Mary is doubly blessed.

Chapter IV
Mary in the Gospel of John

Mary is present in two events recounted by John: at the marriage feast of Cana (2,1-11) and at the crucifixion of Jesus (19,25-27). In Jn 6,42, where the people say that they know the mother and father of Jesus, there is a reference to Mary but she herself does not appear in the scene. Like Mark, John tells us nothing about Jesus' birth. He shows us Mary with her already grown up son. In his Gospel, three distinctive elements are to be noted. First the two scenes where Jesus and Mary appear together are at the beginning and end of his public activity. Secondly the Gospel stresses that she is the Mother of Jesus. Thirdly on both occasions, the disciples of Jesus are involved.

The beginning and the end

At Cana, Jesus changes water into the best wine. As the evangelist explicitly affirms, Jesus worked *"the beginning of his signs "* (2,11), that are so essential for his activity (cf. 20,30-31). From the cross, Jesus unites his Mother to the beloved disciple as a mother to a son. The evangelist adds: *"After this, Jesus, knowing that everything had been accomplished, said..."*(19,28). By uniting his own mother with the disciple, Jesus brought to completion the work that the Father entrusted to him. It is significant that Mary is present at the beginning and the end of Jesus' public ministry. It is from her that the impulse for the first sign comes; the final action that concludes Jesus' public ministry is directed towards her. Both times Mary is present at her own initiative. Even though Mary is not present during the whole of Jesus' public ministry, the beginning and the end show her constant unity with Jesus.

The Mother of Jesus

John underlines in a particular way that Mary is the Mother of Jesus. She is never mentioned by her name but always by the expression "the mother of Jesus" (2,1.3.5.12; 6,42; 19,25.25.26.26.27), ten times in all. John knows the name "Mary" very well and uses it for the sister of Lazarus (11,1-45), for Mary Magdalene (20,1-18) and for another Mary (19,25), but he never uses the name for the Mother of Jesus.

If we did not possess the other gospels, we would not know the name of Jesus' Mother. John puts their relationship in the centre. Mary is differentiated from all other women because she alone is the Mother of Jesus.

John underlines this fact also in another way: apart from the passage in 3,4 where a particular woman is not mentioned but mother in a general sense, the word "mother" is only used for the Mother of Jesus. Mary is the only mother recorded in John's Gospel. Among all mothers, only the mother of Jesus is of interest to the author of this Gospel, and about her the only thing that is mentioned is that she is his mother.

Chapter IV: Mary in the Gospel of John 113

When John speaks about the Mother of Jesus, he does not go into what it means to be a mother. Just as the evangelist presumes that his readers understand the meaning of "bread", "light", "life", "joy" etc, he also presumes that we know what "mother" signifies. However we must understand the significance that his mother had for Jesus and what was their relationship.

Every person exists because he has received human form in the womb of his mother (cf. 3,4) and between a mother and her child there is a unique, enduring relationship. This was so for Jesus and his Mother. She was the mediator of life for Jesus; she accompanied Jesus as he grew up. By speaking of Mary only as "the mother of Jesus", John underlines her importance and her meaning for Jesus and for his entire life.

Connected with the disciples

Wherever Jesus and Mary are together, the disciples also appear. After the sign of Jesus at Cana, the evangelist affirms: "*Jesus accomplished the first of his signs at Cana in Galilee. He manifested his glory and his disciples believed in him*" (2,11). Faith in Jesus is the access to true life and the goal of his whole ministry. This goal is achieved in the disciples, without a doubt based on the sign done by Jesus, which was initiated by Mary. When Jesus accomplished his final work, he united his mother to the beloved disciple (19,26-27). This disciple is also the first to arrive at the empty tomb and to believe (20,8). Mary, who gave earthly life to Jesus, and the disciples, who believing in him have life, belong together.

1. THE MOTHER OF JESUS AT CANA (2,1-12)

From the beginning John focuses attention on the mother of Jesus and his disciples. He writes: *"On the third day there was a marriage feast at Cana in Galilee and the mother of Jesus was there. Jesus was also invited to the wedding along with his disciples "* (2,1-2). Nothing is said about who is getting married. The initiative comes from Mary. Not without some hesitation does Jesus accept her invitation to act but everyone enjoys the fruits of Jesus' action. This is particularly true for Jesus' disciples, who are brought to faith by means of his powerful sign.

Mother of men and women

A mother's task is to see what her children need and employ all her powers in taking care of them. At the marriage feast of Cana, Mary behaves like an attentive and concerned mother. With wide-open eyes, not upon herself but upon what is happening all around her, she becomes aware of a need: they have no more wine. When the wine finishes so does the feast. Without wine, the marriage celebrations must come to an end.

Like a true mother, Mary does not only note the problem, but she seeks to solve it in the best possible way. She cannot solve it herself but she does know someone who can and so she goes to him. What she says to Jesus is only indirectly a question but directly it is a communication concerning the need: *"They have no more wine "*. Mary intercedes in a very reserved

Chapter IV: Mary in the Gospel of John 115

way. She does not wish to force Jesus' hand but respects his freedom. Martha and Mary, the sisters of Lazarus, make a similar request of Jesus: *"Lord, your friend is ill"* (11,3). They too leave Jesus free to decide what to do and they have complete trust in him. Also in this case Jesus does not immediately respond to their request but he does answer their prayer later.

Jesus answers his mother: *"What do I have to do with you, woman? My hour has not yet come"*. By this response Jesus lets his mother know that he feels bound by the will of his Father. It is the Father who has established the hour of the fulfilment of all things and of the glorification of Jesus (cf. 13,1; 17,1), and the Father has determined his whole ministry. If Jesus acts at all, it is not only because he accepts an initiative of his mother, but above all because it is in conformity with the will of God, his Father.

Mary does not understand Jesus' response as a refusal. She tells the servants: *"Do whatever he tells you"*. Jesus himself always puts this at the centre: *"Listen and put into practice the word of God"* (Lk 8,21; 11,25). Mary asks the same of the servants. They must listen to the word of Jesus and act accordingly. Mary goes to Jesus and she leads others to him. They must focus on him and from him they receive their instructions. Mary has complete trust in Jesus and she leaves it to him what to do. She trusts that whatever happens, he will do the right thing.

Like a good mother she takes care of her surroundings. She presents to Jesus the situation of need of these people and invites some to listen to the word of Jesus and follow what he says. She knows who can help, and she helps people by bringing them to Jesus.

The Mother of joy

At the marriage feast of Cana, there is no question of hunger but of feasting and joy. The people present at the celebration do not lack the basic necessities of life but what is running short is wine, which is necessary to continue the feast. Mary gets involved to bring joy and Jesus accomplishes his first "sign" by giving wine in abundance. It is *"the wine that rejoices the human heart"* (Ps 104,15).

Later, in the multiplication of loaves, Jesus gives to the great crowd so much bread that not only are all the people satisfied but there is a lot left over. With this he shows that he is the bread of life and that we can reach the fullness of life by faith in him (6,35). Material bread is needed for our earthly existence that ends in death. Jesus gives eternal, immortal life. Believing in him, which means to recognise him as Son of God, accepting his message as true, placing in him every hope and entrusting ourselves to his guidance, we bind ourselves to him and obtain eternal in him and through him.

In the same way, by means of the gift of wine, Jesus shows that he has come to bring joy that never ends and that, by means of faith in him, we can receive the fullness of joy. In his prayer to the Father, Jesus asks for his disciples *"that they have in themselves the fullness of my joy* " (17,13; cf. 15,11; 16,20-24). Jesus came into the world to bring Good News and joy. His whole work from the very beginning is directed towards this purpose

Mary is the mother of Jesus. Through her came the one who brings the fullness of life and joy to the world. Just as she was at the beginning of Jesus' life, so she was also at the beginning of his public ministry and she gave encouragement to him. In his first great "sign", Jesus revealed himself as he who brings the fullness of joy. The disciples who believe in him participate in his joy and in his life.

2. THE MOTHER OF JESUS UNDER THE CROSS

This is the last action that Jesus accomplishes immediately before his death on the cross. He binds his mother to the beloved disciple as a mother to a son: *"Woman, behold your son. ....Behold your mother."* (19,26-27).

The two people who are closest to Jesus

In the Gospel of John, Jesus' mother and the beloved disciple are characterised by the fact that they are not given a proper name, but are designated by their relationship with Jesus. What is essential to them is not their own name but their relationship with Jesus. The Gospel speaks of "the mother of Jesus". Mary's whole life is determined and characterised by the fact that she is the mother of Jesus. In the same way the Gospel speaks of "the disciple whom Jesus loved"

(13,23; 19,26; 20,2; 21,7.20). According to a very ancient tradition, this person is the apostle and evangelist John. The Gospel does not name him but stresses that he was called to follow Jesus and that the Lord was particularly close to him. Just before Jesus died, he made sure that these two people, who were closest to him, would be bound to each other. It was not their decision but that of Jesus. It is their relationship with Jesus that unites them.

Mary and the disciple as mother and son

In his farewell discourse Jesus had prepared his very sad disciples for his death and for the time following his death (Jn 13-17). He will not leave them orphans. He himself will return to them, and the Father will send them another Consoler, the Spirit of truth (14,16-18). Jesus is concerned also about his mother that she does not remain alone and defenceless. Jesus gives her the beloved disciple as a son. Mary can count on him as on a son. The disciple will respect and love her and will take care of her needs and in the difficulties of old age, as the commandment of God prescribes (Ex 20,12; Mk 7,10). On the other hand, Mary must give him a mother's love, knowing that he is linked closely to Jesus. For the disciple of Jesus, Mary is also his own mother. He must treat her with the love and respect of a son and must have the commitment of a son towards her.

The words of Jesus create a very close bond between his mother and his disciple. From that

Chapter IV: Mary in the Gospel of John

moment they must live for each other. Jesus says to all his disciples: *"Love one another. Just as I have loved you, so you too love one another "* (13,34). This is especially so for Mary and the beloved disciple because to them the love of Jesus has been given in a particular way. Their relationship with Jesus and what they received from him must determine their reciprocal relationship. Precisely because they belong to Jesus in a special way, so they must be bound together in a special way. The love of Jesus and for Jesus does not separate the mother and the disciple but they bind them closely together. The one who knows the love of Jesus and loves Jesus with all his heart is called to love the mother of Jesus and can be sure of her love.

Jesus tells his mother to love the disciple as her own son, just as she has always loved him. Because this is the disciple that Jesus loved in a special way, he asks his mother to accept the disciple as her son for love of him. He asks his disciple to accept Mary as his mother and to love her and take care of her for love of him. What Jesus did was to make sure that his mother was taken care of but that is not all. Jesus creates a bond between the two people who are closest to him. What unites them to him also unites them to each other.

As Mother of Jesus, Mary must be the mother of the disciple. As the disciple that Jesus loved, John must be the son of Mary. Jesus brings his mother into his own relationship with the beloved disciple; he brings his disciple into the relationship he enjoys with his mother. These relationships are part of Jesus' intimate life. By sharing these with others, Jesus is sharing his very self.

He does not reserve for himself a private sphere where no one else may enter. Love for others that takes him to the cross (13,1), is seen by binding his own to each other.

The Mother as mediator of life

Even though the evangelist refers to only one action of the beloved disciple ("*And from that moment the disciple took her into his own*"), it should be clear that the relationship between the mother and the disciple of Jesus is directed toward a gift and a reciprocal acceptance and does not consist only in a unilateral preoccupation of the disciple for Jesus' mother.

In the relationship between a mother and her child, obviously the mother does not only receive. She is the mediator of life. Jesus entered life by means of his mother. The disciple did not receive from Mary his earthly life but he as well as everyone else received Jesus from her. Through him we have all of us received the fullness of life. In this way, Mary is the mother of all and the mediator of life.

The Son of God brings life to us and makes us sharers in his own divine life by taking on flesh (1,14), this mortal life. The fact of having a mother and dying is the most convincing proof that he has become like us. Mary and the cross show that Jesus really shares our human destiny. We can be sure that he is beside us and that with him the immortal life of God has entered into our life. Accepting Mary as the Mother of Jesus, the disciple recognises her as the mediator of his own life.

Chapter IV: Mary in the Gospel of John

At the marriage feast of Cana, Mary showed her motherly attentiveness towards human need. There it also became apparent that she knows Jesus and his power. She leads us to him and leaves to him the decision about what to do. Through the relationship with the Mother of Jesus, the disciple learns to know him even better.

At Cana, on her own initiative, Mary saw the need and sought to do something about it. At the foot of the cross, Jesus invites her to accept the disciple as her own son. Mary must offer to the disciple all her maternal affection and the disciple must represent Jesus for her. She must entrust herself to the love and the care of the disciple, accepting these things from him.

At the centre is Jesus. Everything he does is directed towards the offer of a loving and close relationship. Those who are closest to him become united among themselves. The centre and the goal is communion with him and with God the Father, the origin of all life.

Chapter V
Mary in the Other New Testament Writings

All four Gospels speak of Mary in different measure. In the other writings of the New Testament, the name of Mary is only mentioned one more time. The Acts of the Apostles remember "Mary, the mother of Jesus" within the newborn Church, which is praying for the coming of the Holy Spirit.

Paul, whose letters constitute an important part of the New Testament, speaks once of Mary's important role, without actually naming her. In the letter to the Galatians he writes: *"But when the fullness of time came, God sent His Son, born of woman and subject to the law, in order to rescue those who were subject to the law and so that we would receive adoption as children"* (4,4-5).

Finally we can find in the Apocalypse, the last book of the New Testament, a reference to the mother of Jesus. In a grandiose vision, the Woman is seen, who is about to give birth to the Messiah, and she is threatened by the dragon: *"There appeared a great sign in heaven: a woman, clothed by the sun, with the moon under her feet and on her head a crown of twelve stars. She was pregnant and shouted out in the birth pangs"* (12,1-2). Though our knowledge of Mary comes generally from the Gospels, it is greatly enriched by these passages.

1. Mary in the Primitive Church (Acts 1,14)

The evangelist Luke, in the first two chapters of his Gospel, paints a vivid and varied image of Mary. He mentions her also in his second work, at the beginning of the Acts of the Apostles. The eleven apostles are gathered in the upper room of a house in Jerusalem after the ascension of Jesus and the text goes on: "*All these were assiduous and united in prayer, together with some women and with Mary, the mother of Jesus, and with his brothers*" (Acts 1,14). The whole Church, all those who belonged to the risen Jesus, is gathered together in that one place. Mary, the mother of Jesus, is in their midst and shares in their prayer.

The new born Church

In the first place the eleven apostles belong to the new born Church. They are listed by name; Peter occupies the first place. Jesus has chosen them (Lk 6,13), so that they would accompany him and be able to bear witness to all his words and works. After his resurrection, Jesus appeared before them all; they are to bear witness that he has conquered death and has entered into eternal life with God. The number eleven refers to the fact that their group has an open wound. Jesus called twelve but one of them betrayed him and has disappeared from their circle. Their first action is to close the wound and to appoint another apostle (the twelfth) by lot (Acts 1,15-26).

Among those who have accompanied Jesus throughout Galilee Luke mentions, apart from the

Chapter V: Mary in the other New Testament writings 125

Twelve, some women, *"whom he had healed from evil spirits and from illnesses"* (Lk 8,1-3). These also walked with Jesus and supported him and his disciples with their own means. We meet them again at the foot of the cross (Lk 23,49), at the sepulchre (Lk 23,55) and on the morning of the first Easter (Lk 24, 1-11). They bear witness that Jesus' tomb is empty and they understand that he is alive. They take this news to the apostles who dismiss it as idle gossip but it is wonderfully confirmed with the appearance of the risen Lord. As those who have always been faithful to Jesus and who have participated in the decisive stages of his ministry, they are united with the apostles.

Finally Mary and the brothers of Jesus are mentioned. Luke has mentioned only once in his Gospel this group of Jesus' closest relatives. It is during the public ministry of Jesus and they want to see him. Jesus affirms: *"My mother and my brothers are those who hear the word of God and put it into practice"* (Lk 8,21). Luke has written about Mary, the mother of Jesus, extensively and in a detailed fashion in the first two chapters of the Gospel, presenting her as one who welcomed the word of God and who lived her life based on it.

Other than the apostles, only Mary is mentioned by name and is described explicitly as the mother of Jesus. She is in the midst of those people who were and are closest to Jesus and she has a special place among them. Only Mary is the mother of Jesus. She has known Jesus for the longest time; her whole person and her whole life have been at the service of his coming into the world. According to what Luke says at the beginning of his Gospel, Mary welcomed in faith her task of giving the Messiah to the people of God, and she brought this task to fulfilment in a spirit of total availability and service. She had many things on which to reflect in her heart after the events at the beginning of the Gospel (cf. Lk 2,19.51), and her soul was profoundly wounded as she shared in the rejection met by Jesus (cf. Lk 2,34).

At the centre of the newly born Church is of course Jesus. All the others are present only because they have a close relationship with him. Mary belongs to their group and she brings with her the unique relationship that she had with him. Each member of the Church strengthens the others and they enrich each other in their relationship with Jesus.

The characteristics of the Church

In this circle, Mary can experience how the work of her son was victorious and how it grows. She is part of the Church that has its foundations in the paschal mystery; it is a praying and missionary Church.

Jesus is risen and has been taken up to God, his Father. He now reigns not only over the house of Jacob (Lk 1,33), but also over the whole of heaven and earth. All those gathered in the upper room were profoundly distressed by his death and now are full of joy at his rising from the dead. Mary was not only present at the foot of the cross when Jesus died, but she also experienced the fact that he has conquered death and

Chapter V: Mary in the other New Testament writings 127

has received immortal life from the Father. Those who are gathered are just a small group, around 120 in all (Acts 1,15), but they are those who accompanied Jesus during his life on earth, who encountered him after the resurrection and who know him best. From the witness of these few people come the innumerable host of future Christians.

The command of Jesus has brought them together. He ordered them not to leave Jerusalem, but to wait for what had been promised by the Father, that is the Holy Spirit (Acts 1,4-8). They all obey the command of Jesus and they trust in his promise. They cannot give themselves the Holy Spirit, the divine life, but they can ask for this gift in prayer. Therefore it is said, *"they were assiduous and united in prayer"* (Acts 1,14). In harmony with each other, their hearts are turned towards God. Their prayer reveals their human poverty, but also their trust in the promise of Jesus and their great desire for the Spirit of God. This is the promise of the Father from whom comes all life. Sharing in the divine life involves communion with God, and a conscious and deep bond with the risen Jesus. Through him and in him, they are united with the Father and with all the others. Mary asks for the outpouring of the Spirit along with the others. Luke tells us that Jesus had taught his disciples how to pray (Lk 11,1-13; 18,1-14), but he never shows him praying with them. Mary, on the other hand, is a member of the praying Church.

To this community gathered in prayer, Jesus had given a universal mission: *"You will be my witnesses in*

Jerusalem, and throughout Judea and Samaria, and even to the ends of the earth " (Acts 1,8). These people had met Jesus and through him had encountered God in a new way. This experience, however, is not confined to them. They are still a small group and this one place in Jerusalem is sufficient for them. What has been given to them must reach, through them, the whole world, which must be filled with the joy of the resurrection and by the Holy Spirit. An integral part of this message is the way in which the all-powerful God has acted in and through Mary. The diffusion of the message is accompanied also by the fact that all generations will call Mary blessed (Lk 1,48-49).

Mary and the Church

Mary and the Church have many things in common. Both have been chosen, in different ways, to bring to the world the Messiah, through whom God brings about the work of salvation. Neither can do this relying on their own strength, but they depend on the Holy Spirit. By means of the Spirit, Jesus began his life in Mary (Lk 1,35). Only by means of the Holy Spirit can the young Church obtain the clarity and the courage to announce to the world that Jesus is risen (Acts 2). Both Mary and the Church take up their task in faith (Lk 1,45) and they seek God and the divine assistance in prayer (Acts 1,14). God calls both to the service of the whole of humanity.

As the mother of Jesus, Mary is called to a particular service of Jesus and the people of God. To her is also granted the greatest closeness to Jesus. Mary was able to participate in the life of Jesus from the beginning until the announcement to the whole of Israel. Both for Mary and for the Church, the bond with Jesus is essential. The life of Jesus began within the womb of Mary and there also begins the possibility of other people coming into communion with him. Mary belongs to the Church, that is to the people who believe in Jesus and who live with him. In this Church the mother of Jesus has a very special task and place.

2. THE MOTHER OF GOD'S OWN SON

The letters of St. Paul are believed to be the first of the New Testament writings. The Apostle sent them between the years 50-60 to various Christian communities. They concentrate on the meaning of the coming of Jesus Christ into the world and of his death and resurrection. They are also concerned with certain problems regarding living the Christian life. Only rarely do they record some particular of the life of Jesus. The name of Mary, the mother of Jesus, is not mentioned in the letters. However, Paul speaks once about the birth of the Son of God from a woman and by implication refers to the mother of Jesus.

In the letter to the Galatians, composed probably between 53 and 55 A.D., St. Paul writes: *"But when the fullness of time came, God sent His Son, born of a woman and subject to the Law, in order to redeem those who were under the Law and so that they would receive adoption as His children "* (Gal 4,4-5). Here not even the name of Jesus is mentioned, but the essential characteristics of his person and of his coming into the world are presented. He is the Son of God who lives from all eternity in communion with God the Father. In the fullness of time, determined by God, he was sent into the world by the Father. He was born of a woman just like any human being, and therefore he accepted what it means to be human. As a member of the people of God, he was subject to the Law but the goal of his coming into the world was to redeem everyone from under the Law and give them the possibility to become children of God. He comes from the fullness of life with God and he must conquer sin and death. He desires to take everyone with him and lead them to share in his life as Son in communion with God the Father.

Even though he does not mention the name of Mary and says nothing about the precise circumstances of her maternity, Paul communicates the essentials to us. His brief reference to Mary, which is the oldest witness, expresses at the same time, in the clearest possible way, her task and dignity: Mary is the Mother of God's own Son. The Gospels report details and show a vibrant image of Mary, but even they cannot say anything more important than the fact that Mary is the mother of the Son of God. That God destined her for this role is a fundamental and immutable reality and precedes anything she did. Mary must respond to this divine decree in faith and with her whole life. What characterises Mary above all is this task and this position that God has assigned her. God does not act without human cooperation. Mary has a special place in the divine plan of salvation; through her, God sends

Chapter V: Mary in the other New Testament writings

His Son into the world to lead to the fullness of life humanity that was subject to death.

The love of God the Father for a lost humanity

The work in which Mary has her place comes from God the Father and is determined by divine love. God created the world and human beings. God called Abraham and through him established and chose the people of Israel. People in general, including Israel, do not recognise their Creator and do not give homage to God. They rebel against and separate themselves from God, and they let themselves be guided by their desires. Whoever owes his or her life to God – and all things come from God – cannot find the fullness of life outside of God or in opposition to God. To act in opposition to God means the destruction of one's own life. Those who do not follow God choose death. How does God act in these circumstances? Does God abandon those who have been created with free will, to the destruction that has been freely chosen, to emptiness and to lack of meaning?

The greatness of God and the extent of divine love are shown in the fact that God does not leave human beings to their own devices. God's action is not determined by human response or lack of it. There is no tit for tat response. God remains faithful to the divine nature, and acts always in goodness and love. God responds to indifference on the part of human beings with new gifts. To those who have chosen death, God offers an even higher form of life: communion with God. God does not hate unfaithful and evil people, but desires to bring them into an even closer sharing in the divine life.

The New Testament bears witness in many ways to God's love for ungrateful people. Jesus declares his mission to be: *"I have not come to call the just but sinners to repentance "* (Mk 2,17). In the letter to the Romans, Paul writes: *"But God has shown love for us because while we were still sinners, Christ died for us "* (Rom 5,8). John affirms in his first letter: *"In this has been demonstrated the love of God for us: God has sent His only Son into the world, so that we might have life through him. In this love consists: it is not us who have loved God, but it is God who has loved us and sent His Son as a victim of expiation for our sins "* (1 Jn 4, 9-10).

In the beginning is God and the divine love. God remains continually the One who determines all things. God created the world and sent His Son for us sinners. Because of God's love for us, we have been given, through the Son, the fullness of life.

The mission of the Son of God

In Galatians 4, 4-5, Paul records only in what conditions the Son of God came into the world. He was born of a woman and subject to the Law. In other passages the Apostle explains from where Jesus comes and what brought about his coming into the world. In the letter to the Philippians he writes: *"Though he was equal to God, he did not hold fast to this equality as to a treasure, but he emptied himself to take on the condition of a slave and became similar to all people. He appeared in human form and abased himself by becoming obedient even to death, death on a cross"* (Phil 2, 6-8). The Son's point of departure is His communion with the Father. He is equal to the Father and shares the divine life fully and with an unimaginable beatitude. In obedience to the Father, he leaves this divine life to become a man and to share with men and women all aspects of human life even to death, which for him was a violent death on the cross. The Father sent him into the world, which is subject to violence and death and which has become evil. He accepted this mission for love of his Father.

What is asked of the Son and what he gives to people, Paul describes in this way: *"You know what Jesus Christ has done because of his love: being rich, he became poor for you, so that you might become rich by means of his poverty"* (2 Cor 8,9). For love of human beings, God sent the Son, who also loves the human race.

By his coming there is a wonderful exchange. The Son takes on and shares in the poverty of human life, in order to make us share in the fullness of life, from which he comes and which he has in common with the Father.

For Paul the decisive event is that in Jesus Christ the Son of God has come into the world. Everything is decided and given by the Father by means of this mission of the Son. For Paul personally the gift of grace par excellence is the fact that God revealed the Son to him (Gal 1,15-16). The central content of all

Paul's work is to proclaim the Good News regarding the Son of God (Rom 1,3.9; Gal 1, 16). This Good News fills the Apostle himself with unending wonder and an infinite joy. From this core come all the other elements of his preaching. This is the Good News that Paul feels compelled to bring to all people, Jews and pagans. Until the coming of Jesus Christ, God left human beings with the world, with the Law, with their sins and with their evil opposition to the divine plan. It was uncertain whether we could act justly in relation to God, who is the origin and goal of all life. Now the Son of God is forever beside us as a sign of the infinite love of God, who has never and will never cease to love us and be concerned with the course of our lives. We are no longer abandoned to ourselves or alone with other creatures. The Son of God is with us; we can depend on him and through him, we can infallibly come to God and respond to God's love.

The fruit of Jesus' coming into the world

Paul synthesises in the following way what God gives us through the coming of the Son: *"Faithful is God, by whom you have been called into communion with His Son Jesus Christ, our Lord!"* (I Cor 1,9). The Son is characterised by his communion with the Father. He shares in the life of the Father, infinite and having the fullness of divinity. He is one with the Father in an unlimited and reciprocal knowledge and love. Communion with the Son means also communion with the Father; it means being children of God in the Son. Starting from the position of distance and going further away towards death and disaster, we are called to communion and to closeness, to life with the Father, which is an infinitely blessed life. This meaning of the coming of Jesus into the world is expressed by Paul in the letter to the Galatians: *"God sent His Son ...... so that we might receive adoption as children"* (Gal 4,4-5).

We enter into communion with Jesus Christ and we become children of God, when we believe in Jesus as the Son of God. To believe means recognising that the relationship of Jesus to God is one of Son to Father, and then entrusting ourselves to him and seeking his guidance. It means placing one's life in his hands and allowing ourselves to be directed by him, directing to him all our hopes and expectations. Paul describes our access to this relationship when he writes: *"All of you are children of God through faith in Christ Jesus, because inasmuch as you are baptised in Christ, you are clothed in Christ. There is no more Jew or Greek; there is no more slave or free; no more man or woman, because all of you are one in Christ Jesus "* ((Gal 3, 26-28). The baptism that we receive as an expression of faith in Jesus, the Son of God, binds us to him in the closest possible way and makes us children of God. This relationship is so decisive that all other essential qualities of a person – be they from the history of salvation (cf. Gal 2,15), social or sexual – recede in its wake. Everything else takes second place to this relationship that is common to all the baptised: God is my Father and I am His child through His Son, Jesus Christ.

This relationship not only is to be experienced as present but it is to be lived in the most conscious and active way possible: *"And that you are children is proved by the fact that God has sent into our hearts the Spirit of His Son, who cries out: Abba, Father! Therefore you are no longer a slave but a son or daughter; and if you are a son or daughter, you are also an heir, by the will of God"* (Gal 4,6-7). The same God who sends the Son into the world, sends the Spirit also into the very centre of our being, into our hearts. It is the same Spirit that filled the heart of God's Son. Through this Spirit we are brought into the closest possible relationship with the Father. A sign of this is that spontaneously and clearly as sons and daughters we call God "Father". As children of God, we are also God's heirs, inheriting everything that belongs to God. By means of the Son, Jesus Christ, and the Spirit, God introduces us into all that pertains to the divine life.

The woman who gave birth to the Son of God

In this event that comes from God, in which through the mission of the Son of God all people are called to the fullness of life and blessing, one woman has the task of being mother to this Son. For his coming into the world the Son of God follows the normal way of every human being. He takes form in the womb of his mother and is born from her. For years he depends totally on her loving care, in order to be able to develop his own capabilities and become an adult.

Paul refers only to the fact that the Son of God was born of a woman. He never mentions the name of this woman, and neither does the Gospel of John. He says nothing about the circumstances surrounding the conception and birth of the child, and nothing about the relationship between mother and son. Paul does not reflect on what this role means from God's point of view, or what are its implications.

In the passages in which Paul reflects on his own task as an apostle, we find some ideas of this nature. He presents himself as: *"Paul, the servant of Christ Jesus, called to be an apostle, chosen to announce the Good News from God"* (Rom 1,1). He has been chosen and called by God for this task. In the letter to the Galatians, in which he records the birth of the Son of God from a woman, Paul briefly describes his own vocation, which was given him through the revelation of God's Son. Here he speaks of *"God, who chose me from my mother's womb and called me by grace"* (Gal 1, 15-16). The Apostle explains that this vocation belongs to his very existence from the very beginning and that it is a particular gift of God's love.

If we see the way in which Paul understands his own role, we cannot possibly think that he would consider the mother of God's Son as an impersonal instrument, insignificant to the divine plan. Everything suggests that he understands the role of Mary, that certainly is on another level, in a way that corresponds to his own role and that he recognises her as beloved and chosen by God. However the fact remains that Paul does not explicitly express this idea and that in his writings there is nothing comparable to Luke 1, 26-38.

Paul gives us the briefest and most ancient reference to the woman who gave birth to the Son of

God. He also defines in a precise and complete way the whole picture within which Mary brings her task to completion. Through the Son, God reveals that he is in fact community. This is the most alive and welcoming community possible. The Father sends the Son to set us free from perdition and introduces us into the divine life. Mary is the woman through whom the Son of God comes into the world to accomplish this task. With this woman he lives in communion as he grows in preparation for his task. Of her nothing greater can be said than that she is the mother of the Son of God. It is still important what Luther said: "*It is necessary to ponder in one's heart what it means that she is the mother of God*". Paul affirms this reality but does not draw out its implications.

3. MARY, THE SIGN IN HEAVEN (APOC 12, 1-6)

The Gospels and the Acts of the Apostles speak explicitly about Mary and refer to particular events of her life. In the book of Apocalypse 12,1-2, we read: "*In heaven there appeared a great sign: a woman clothed in the sun, with the moon beneath her feet and on her head a crown of twelve stars. She was pregnant and cried out with the pains of childbirth* ". Here we are not treating of a particular historical event; in this vision certain essentials are expressed and brought together. Does this image refer only to the people of God from whom came the Messiah or does it also refer to the woman who gave birth to him? It is true that in this image of the pregnant woman we can contemplate the people of God but it is equally true that we can also contemplate the figure of the woman who brought the Messiah into the world. As the mother of the Messiah, Mary is the personification of the people of God, and the particular elements of the vision speak also of her.

The woman in heavenly glory

The most beautiful heavenly bodies are employed to adorn this woman, in order to manifest her position and dignity. Everything in her is light and brightness, beauty and adornment. The greatest and brightest heavenly body, the sun itself, is used to clothe her. She is surrounded in a dazzling light. She stands upon the moon and her crown is made up of twelve glittering stars. No other earthly reality is so luminous and splendid as these heavenly bodies. No human being can use these and take them for ornament. From the first moment of her appearance we can see that this woman is splendid and completely pure and that she has received everything from God. Only God could have given her such beauty. Some time after this vision, another figure is described: *"The woman was clothed in purple and scarlet and adorned with gold, precious stones and pearls"* (Apoc 17,4). This woman has nothing from God; she has clothed herself with all the jewels that human beings use. However, all these pale in the face of the heavenly splendour.

The aspect of the first woman tells us something of her role and of her position. The sun, with its blazing splendour and its consuming fire, refers to God and the divine glory. The woman carries in her womb a child, who immediately after his birth is taken up to God and the heavenly throne (Apoc 12,5). Because of her child, she is the mother of God, and so she is clothed with the sun. The art of the Eastern Church has images of Mary as a burning bush (cf Ex 3,2). Since the Son of God is present in her, she is surrounded by fire but not consumed.

The crown of twelve stars points her out as queen within the people of God. The number twelve refers to the people of God based on the symbols of the twelve tribes of the children of Israel (cf. Apoc 7,5-8; 21,12) and the twelve apostles of the Lamb (Apoc 21,16). Mary gives a very special service to the people of God by giving life to its king. Therefore within this people she has a very particular place and dignity. All must treat her with respect and gratitude.

The moon is different from the sun not only because of its much weaker light but also because it is changeable. The fact that the woman is above the moon shows her as unchangeable and entirely trustworthy; she is and remains forever the mother of God's Son. She can never lose her splendour and dignity.

The Mother of the Lord and Saviour

We see this woman full of splendour but at the same time she is in a condition that makes her weak and places her in danger. For her has come the most important and difficult hour: "*She was pregnant and cried out with the pains of childbirth...... She gave birth to a male child, who was destined to govern all the nations with a sceptre of iron. And her son was immediately taken up towards God and His throne "* (Apoc 12,2.5).

The most difficult moment for the woman is also her greatest. It is the time in which she fulfils her principal task of being a mother by bearing her child. All the attention is placed on the fact that the woman has given birth to this child, while all the details regarding her relationship with her son are in second place. The task and the special position of Mary are constituted by the fact that she is the mother of this child. Every splendour and every privilege come from this fact and are directed towards it.

The Gospel of Matthew always uses the expression "the child and his mother". The Gospel of John never uses the name "Mary", but speaks always of "the mother of Jesus". The Apocalypse puts in the first place the birth itself. Thus at the centre is the fact that Mary is the Mother of Jesus.

Also only the most important thing is communicated regarding the son: he is not only the king of God's people, but also the Lord of all. He has his special place of honour beside God. With him, one who was born of a woman (cf Gal 4,4), and who is truly human, has entered definitively into God's realm. By means of its king and Lord, humanity has attained its goal, which is communion with God and the fullness of divine life. Mary is the mother of the conqueror and saviour; her son opens to every human being access to life with God.

The sign in heaven

The woman is described explicitly as "a great sign in heaven". For the ancients, the stars were vital for guiding them on their journeys on the sea and in the desert. The sign of the woman is to give us direction on the journey of our life.

Beside her appears another sign: "*An enormous red dragon, with seven heads and ten horns and on its heads seven diadems*" (Apoc 12,3). The dragon is identified as "*the ancient serpent, he who is called the devil and satan, the one who seduces the whole earth.*" (Apoc 12,9). It's great size, power, terrifying aspect, aggressiveness and menace are emphasised. The dragon stands in front of the woman who is about to give birth and wishes to devour the child. It threatens the woman herself. It threatens "*all those who observe the commandments of God and possess the testimony of Jesus*" (Apoc 12,17). The child and the woman are saved from the influence of the dragon by the power of God. The other members of the people of God are involved in a struggle with it and with its allies. They are under pressure and subject to temptation. It is not sure whether they will remain faithful to God and attain their end, which is communion with God.

In this situation the sign of the woman must give courage and continually point out the right way. Mary is the mother. She welcomed the call of God and accepted to put herself at the service of her child and the whole people of God. Therefore she is surrounded by the splendour of God and is under the powerful

Chapter V: Mary in the other New Testament writings 143

divine protection. Through her, it is clear that God gives strength and protects. The figure contrasted to Mary is that of the prostitute, who belongs to the dragon and sits on a beast that serves it (Apoc 17,3-6; cf. 13,1). The prostitute rejects any relationship and any form of service. She lives for herself and wastes her life, throwing it away in a frantic pursuit of pleasure and unrestrained luxury. She blasphemes against God and is heading for ruin.

Both signs are very clear. While we live we must choose which sign to follow. Mary stands for relationship and service, for communion with God and the acceptance of divine protection. The dragon and the prostitute stand for complete liberty to follow one's selfish impulses, for separation from God and for solitude without hope.

Chapter VI
Mary in the New Testament

Only a few passages in the New Testament speak of Mary. We have sought to listen to the witness they give in the most attentive and precise way possible. It can be surprising to see just how much these have to say on Mary's vocation from God, on her experience with Jesus, her relationship with him when he was a child and during his public ministry, and on her relationship with his disciples. We do not intend to list the numerous particular aspects that make up the vivid and complex portrait of Mary. By way of conclusion, it might be worthwhile to indicate what characteristics of Mary each passage presents and what qualities of Mary are at the basis of all the particular elements.

1. The images of Mary

In the world of art, different kinds of images are produced according to the style and technique used. In drawing, the artist produces the most important characteristics of a figure with a few broad strokes. An oil painting has fewer clear edges but has greater possibility to present the atmosphere of a scene. A very precise picture is interesting in that it contains many details. However, every type of representation has its limits in that it chooses only certain points from the infinite wealth of reality and leaves other elements aside without denying or negating them. The interest, capacity and knowledge of the artist guide the choice of topic and how it is executed.

In the writings of the New Testament, we find various images of Mary that are clearly differentiated according to content and modes of expression. We do not wish to paper over these distinctions in order to compose a single composite figure. Each element should be taken on its own and allowed to speak to us in its own way. To the reader of the New Testament has been given the possibility of getting to know the mother of Jesus through each image and so acquire a profound and life-giving knowledge of her.

a) Matthew: the service of the Virgin Mother

Matthew is the only evangelist who begins his work with the genealogy of Jesus, in which he mentions Mary as the wife of Joseph and the mother of Jesus. From the beginning he describes Jesus as the heir and the one who brings to fulfilment the history of God's dealings with the people of Israel and demonstrates Mary's place in the history of salvation. God destined her to be the virgin mother of the Christ, through whom God sets Israel and the whole of humanity free from the slavery of sin, bringing them into divine intimacy.

The one whose task it is to bind humanity to God in a complete way comes absolutely from God. With the background of a long series of human generations and breaking the chain, Matthew underlines that Jesus had no human father. He began his human life in Mary's womb by the power of the Holy Spirit. The evangelist

Chapter VI: Mary in the New Testament 147

tells us nothing about how Mary became aware of her role and how she accepted it. The point that Matthew wants to make is that everything comes from God who chose her. God called Mary and by means of the divine creative power, made her capable of becoming the mother of Christ. God assigned to her the task of being, for Israel and for the whole of humanity, the mother of the Saviour, Emmanuel (God with us).

Matthew also stresses the task for which Joseph was called into service. He was to take Mary as his wife and give a name to the baby. Through him, the legal father, Jesus was legitimately inserted into the genealogy. By his protection and concern, Joseph provides the human structures within which Mary can be faithful to her maternal vocation. With the expression, repeated several times, "the child and his mother", the evangelist wants to refer to a close communion of life between Mary and Jesus. The baby depends on his mother and she is there for him with her whole heart and strength.

Matthew never mentions what Mary thought, felt or said. Her personal experience is excluded from his sober exposition. He puts Mary's service and motherhood at the centre of the picture. She is mother through the work of the Holy Spirit and is completely dedicated to her child, at the service of his coming into the world and of his human growth. She serves the people of God, to whom she brings the Saviour.

b) Mark: the care of the Mother for her Son

Among all the evangelists Mark is the one who

communicates least about Mary. Once only she is present along with the brothers of Jesus. They are very concerned about Jesus and they want to take him home. Jesus refuses to receive them and rejects their preoccupation for him. He makes clear that the only way to be in relationship with him is to do the will of God (Mk 3, 21.31-35). It seems that Mark is only aware of or interested in the conflict between Jesus and his family. They want to protect his life while he wants to fulfil his mission without regard for his own life. Seemingly Jesus distances himself from his mother and other relatives and establishes a new "family" with the disciples who followed him. It seems that his family do not take his mission seriously and belong more to his enemies than to his followers.

Using a very dubious opinion and explanation of this text, some people consider the conflict between Jesus and Mary as the only secure historical element that we can know about their relationship. Moreover, Mark, for what he says and does not say, is made the criterion of everything else, and the other Gospels and what they have to say about Mary are judged by this. Mark speaks only of this conflict and says nothing about the virginal conception of Jesus for example. He presents none of the positive aspects of Mary found in the Gospels of Luke, Matthew and John.

Based only on what Mark says and does not say, the following picture of Mary is sometimes built up: she conceived Jesus in the natural way by Joseph; she had other sons and daughters and Jesus grew up in Nazareth as one of a large family; until his public ministry there was nothing exceptional about him; Mary did not know about the task for which Jesus was destined and so she was completely surprised when he left the family and by his understanding of his mission; unlike the disciples who accepted his claims, believed in him and followed him, the family of Jesus – including Mary – were sceptical about his mission or even rejected it; only after the resurrection of Jesus were they united with the disciples. Someone has even gone so far as to suggest that Mary was never a member of the Church. The testimony of the other Gospels is considered as not historical and as a pious invention.

Certainly Mark shows in a particularly clear way that there was a conflict between Jesus and his family but the tension between what Jesus did and the experience of his mother is referred to also by the other evangelists (Mt 12,46-50; Lk 2,35.48-50; Jn 2,4) and is placed among the positive traits of Mary.

Regarding the understanding of the conflict in Mark, it is necessary to point out at least two things. Firstly this conflict cannot be interpreted as an absolute distancing of Jesus from his mother. Secondly it can only be correctly evaluated within the overall thrust of Mark's Gospel.

The behaviour of Jesus in Mk 3,31-35 is certainly a challenge for his mother (cf. Lk 2,41-52) but it is not a rejection or condemnation. Jesus challenges Mary and shows her what she must do. Mark does not tell us Mary's reaction and therefore leaves open the possibility that she accepted the challenge and grew because of it.

We should not ignore either that here we are dealing with a conflict between two people who are closely united. Mary's going to Jesus demonstrates her maternal concern and her relationship with him. As regards Jesus there can be no doubt that he is very close to her. In Mk 6,3, he is named as "son of Mary"; he is profoundly connected to her and through her he is rooted in Nazareth. Also in Mark's Gospel Jesus underlines the importance of the fourth commandment and insists on its absolute validity as the word of God (Mk 7,6-13; Mt 15,3-9). Therefore it is impossible that Jesus, who demanded with such force the fulfilment of God's will (Mk 3,35) did not respect his own mother and treat her in an exemplary way. Certainly the will of God takes precedence over everything else and Jesus must remain faithful to his mission. He cannot avoid causing bitter suffering to his mother. However with the same level of certainty, the fourth commandment remains valid and Jesus is bound to his mother with a singular love and gratitude, based on the will of his Father.

More than the others, Mark brings to light in his Gospel the contrast between the human will and the will of God. He stresses how much the way of Jesus that leads to the resurrection through suffering and death, is contrary to human nature. Jesus must walk this path (Mk 8,31), which is according to the Scriptures (Mk 9,12-13; 14,21) and the will of God (Mk 8,33; 14,36). On this path, faith in the mission of Jesus and in his awareness of the will of God is severely tested. To attain the fullness of life (resurrection) we must give up blindly and without guarantee the life that we have and to which we are so attached. This requires a pure and blind faith.

Mark conceived his Gospel in this way and shows that everyone is inadequate when confronted with Jesus and his way. By means of this insufficiency of human beings, the divine source of the claim and the work of Jesus is revealed. What he is and does goes beyond human criteria and understanding. The rejection by the enemies of Jesus demonstrates just how much the claim of Jesus was unheard of (Mk 2,7; 3,22.30; 14,60-64). Even those who belong to Jesus cannot grasp the significance of his mission and are constantly challenged to enlarge and deepen their faith. This is the situation for Jesus' family but also for his disciples, and, at the end, is the case for the women who accompany him to the cross and the tomb. Mark presents all of this in a coherent way.

The relatives of Jesus see his life threatened because of what he is doing and they want to take him to the safety of Nazareth. Jesus rejects this plan, refers to the will of God and asks them to make this their own.

The disciples heard from Jesus the first announcement of his passion, death and resurrection (Mk 8,31). Peter, speaking on behalf of the rest, opposes this and raises a strong protest (Mk 8,32). His awareness that Jesus is the Christ (Mk 8,29) does not stop him and even encourages him. Jesus rejects him in the most severe way possible and he says: "*You do not think according to God, but in a human way*" (Mk 8,33). The ways that both Peter and the relatives of Jesus act, and how Jesus responds to them, correspond in the details. In both cases, those who are closest to Jesus intervene because they understand that his life is threatened. In both cases Jesus strongly rejects their suggestions and appeals to the will of God. Always the spontaneous desire of human beings is contrasted to the will of God, which Jesus knows and that for him constitutes the decisive criterion. Starting from this clash, a contrast opens up between Jesus and his disciples. They continue to follow him and he instructs them right up to his last evening, which he spends only with them (Mk 14,12-42). However they are not on Jesus' wavelength (cf. Mk 9,32-34; 10,35-41) and this gap leads to their running away when Jesus is arrested (Mk 14,50), and to Peter's denial (Mk 14,66-72). The disciples are not at the level of Jesus and cannot understand his way. They need the risen Lord to re-establish communion with himself (Mk 14,28; 16,7).

The women who follow Jesus even to the foot of the cross (Mk 15,40-41), help with his burial (Mk 15,47), and go to the tomb on Easter morning, seem to have the right understanding of Jesus, more so than his own family and disciples. However Mark also shows their limits. These also have failed to grasp completely the explanation of Jesus about the way destined for him by God; for them also the resurrection is an idea that is empty of meaning. The women go to the tomb to anoint a dead body and they are completely astounded by the message of the resurrection (Mk 16,6-8). These too are human beings and they cannot comprehend the action of God.

The tension between human expectations and desires on the one hand, and what is God's will on the other, can be seen in Jesus himself and this is particularly brought out by Mark. In Gethsemane, Jesus prays: *"Abba, Father. Everything is possible for you. Take this chalice away from me! Yet, not what I will but what you will "* (Mk 14,36). He repeats this prayer a second time (14,39). Jesus expresses his human desire to be released from death but he submits himself completely to the will of the Father. This tension also manifests itself at the moment of his death when he says, *"My God, my God, why have you abandoned me?"* (Mk 15,34). For Jesus, the Father is and remains his God, to whom he is inseparably bound. With great firmness Jesus trusts the Father. However, according to his immediate human feelings, he experiences abandonment by the Father. Jesus is truly human and he has a natural and lively repugnance for suffering and death. Also for Jesus it requires effort and commitment to regulate his life completely according to the will of his Father. We can see this in the way he acts in Gethsemane (Mk 14,32-42; cf. Jn 12,27-33; Heb 5,5-10).

All of this might make us think that we had moved away from our theme of Mary in Mark's Gospel. However we cannot correctly understand the tense encounter between Jesus and his family (Mk 3,31-35) if we take it in isolation. It is necessary to judge this scene within the context of the whole of Mark's Gospel. For this reason we have presented the principal argument of this Gospel.

In this way it becomes possible to correct two dubious interpretations. If Mk 3,31-35 showed a profound split between Jesus and his mother, and that Mary had no understanding of her son's mission, tried to block his way and was scolded by him, and if this scene were indeed the explanation of all the material in the other Gospels, then it would mean that this passage would have to be explained in an abstract fashion without any reference to the wider context. There is no solid ground for this idea. On the other hand Mk 3,31-35 shows the suggestion to be false that would claim a relationship between Jesus and Mary that was always serene and free of all problems and tensions and that Mary always understood her son completely. The encounter shows that, despite a strong bond, there was still quite a distance between Jesus and his mother and how he challenged her to go further and grow in her faith in order to fulfil the will of God.

It is to misunderstand Mark's Gospel to think that he wishes to set up an opposition against the mother and other relatives of Jesus. The evangelist does not do this just as he does not do it with regard to the disciples. The tension between Jesus and his mother – and every human feeling, even in Jesus himself – shows that the path taken by him and his work were completely new and unheard of. What he was doing and what he was claiming was contrary to human experience and expectations. Through the various inadequate human reactions, the super human character of the person and mission of Jesus is made clear. Also the need to grow in faith is stressed and this applies equally to Mary.

In the few details that Mark transmits concerning Mary and her relationship with Jesus, he reveals a whole world. In Mary's concern for the life of her son we see expressed her profound maternal bond with him.

According to the measure and intensity of this bond, Mary is involved in his mission and is challenged to accept the will of God and to continue growing in faith. Through her son, she too is put on the road to a process of growth and maturation that would involve great suffering. What Mark says of Mary accords with what we learn of her from the other Gospels.

c) **Luke: mother and listener to the Word of God**

Simply from the number of texts in which Mary is mentioned we can see that there is a great difference among the Gospels. In Mt there are 54 verses (1,1-2,23; 12,46-50; 13,55; in Mk 7 verses (3,21. 31-35; 6,3); in Lk 88 verses (1,26-56; 2,1-52; 8,19-21; 11,27-28); and in Jn there are 16 verses (2,1-12; 6,42; 19,25-27). It is simple to see that Lk has the greater number of texts. From this results that more than half of our explanations focus on Luke's Gospel.

Luke gives us most detail about Mary. Of this, much belongs to the particular nature of his image of her. Only the third evangelist tells us that her name is "Mary" (12 times). He uses the term "mother" 7 times. This does not seem to be by chance but is a consequence of the fact that Luke, almost alone, speaks of the personal experience of Mary. He records her perplexity, her reflection, questioning, consent, faith, praise and jubilation. He speaks of her soul and her spirit (1,26-56). Luke tells us that she has kept in her heart all the events in which she has been involved (2,19.51) and that her soul is wounded with sorrow (2,35.49). Luke's Gospel shows her as one who has a lively relationship with God (1,26-56) and in a difficult encounter with her 12 year old son (2,41-52). Only Lk takes account of this personal experience of Mary.

Only in Luke's Gospel do we find other people directing their attention to Mary, and they take up a position in regard to her. Elizabeth, inspired by the Holy Spirit, recognised her as the mother of the Lord, blessed in a special way by God. Elizabeth declares that Mary is blessed because of her faith (Lk 1,39-45). Simeon, also moved by the Holy Spirit, announces to Mary that the opposition to her son will profoundly wound her soul (Lk 2,25-35). A woman in the crowd declares her blessed to be the mother of such a son (Lk 11,27). With a prophetic prediction, Mary herself affirmed that all generations would call her blessed because of the great things God had done in her. Only here does Luke's gaze (and that of the reader) go beyond the actual life of Mary towards an unlimited future. Luke also mentions Mary after the resurrection of Jesus and shows her within the young Church in the Acts of the Apostles.

In the image that Matthew gives of Mary, everything is concentrated on the task that God has assigned to her, to be the virgin mother of His Son. Mary remains limited to the relationship with her son and with Joseph. Luke adds to this her own personal experience, the way in which she accepted her task, carried it out and lived it. Mary also stands in a wider circle of relationships and receives unlimited attention throughout the course of history. Even in this image of Mary that is very rich and reveals many aspects of her personality, central is the

Chapter VI: Mary in the New Testament

way that God acts in her regard. At the centre of Mary's action is her response to God.

All the times that Mary is mentioned, the action of God in her regard takes precedence. First of all, God's messenger says: *"Rejoice, full of grace, the Lord is with you!"* (Lk 1,28). What characterises Mary, like a name, is the fact that God has made her full of grace, worthy of the divine love and benevolence. God is the one who entrusts to her the task of being the mother of the Messiah and makes her capable of doing so through an act of divine creative power. Elizabeth also affirms above all: *"God has blessed you more than all other women"* (Lk 1,42). Mary will be called blessed by all generations because the Almighty has done great things in her (Lk 1,48-49). There is no doubt that everything comes as a gift from God.

Mary's response in regard to God is summed up by her when she calls herself *"the servant of the Lord"* (Lk 1,38.48). As the servant she listens to the word of the Lord and she seeks God's will. This attitude is determined by faith in the Lord and in God's word. Elizabeth characterises Mary's attitude in this way and for this reason declares her blessed (Lk 1,45). Just how much Mary is directed towards the Lord, His word, and all that comes from God, is seen also in the fact that she keeps all these things in her heart and meditates on them (Lk 2,19). Finally, this attitude of Mary is seen in her perfect keeping of the law of the Lord (Lk 2,21-24.39.41). With this disposition she fulfils her task of being the virgin mother of the Messiah and cares for the upbringing of her son.

When Mary was once more in Jerusalem for the feast of the Passover and her son was at the beginning of his adulthood, she was asked to take another step forward in her listening to the Lord. Jesus based himself totally on the will of his Father for his surprising way of acting that gave such pain (Lk 2,49). In this way he announced beforehand that in the future the word and the will of God will come to Mary in the words and action of her son and must be accepted by her. Mary does not understand Jesus (Lk 2,50) but continues her previous attitude. Just as she pondered in her heart the events of God (Lk 2,19), so now she does the same thing when faced with the words and actions of her son (Lk 2,51). Mary would like to understand but she knows to wait in love and patience while maintaining an unconditional faith in the guidance of God and the unconditional communion with her son.

When Mary is mentioned during Jesus' public ministry, it is always in a context of listening to the word of God that is communicated to her through the Son of God (Lk 8,21; 11,28). This word is rightly received by those who *"after having heard the word with good and perfect hearts, observe it and produce fruit through their perseverance "* (Lk 8,15). As the servant of the Lord, and as one who keeps in her heart everything that happened (Lk 2,19.51), she has patience. She has to use these attitudes and put into practice the word of God that comes to her through her son (cf. Lk 2,48-51).

The vocation of Mary is to be the Mother of the Messiah and then the one who listens to His word. This

Chapter VI: Mary in the New Testament

is reflected in the passage in Luke's Gospel where the figure of Mary appears for the last time (11,27-28). A woman in the crowd declares her blessed because she is the mother of Jesus. He declares blessed all those who listen to the word of God. In faith and as the servant of the Lord, Mary became the mother of the Messiah. She gave to the people of God the one who manifested to all (including to Mary herself) the definitive will of God and brought the fullness of life. Mary alone is the mother of Jesus and as such she has a particular relationship with him. Along with all the other members of the people of God, Mary listens to Jesus, and she is found at the centre of the Church praying for the gift of the Holy Spirit (Acts 1,14). Mary is not limited to being the mother of Jesus, but accepts him also as her own Messiah. She does not cease to be the mother of Jesus but in a special way she is guided by his word and his mission.

From the very beginning the relationship of Mary with God and her relationship with Jesus are bound up together in the closest possible way. This relationship does not always remain the same but develops. Called by God, and by means of the divine creative power, Mary becomes the mother of Jesus in faith as the servant of the Lord. She remains always the one who believes. In regard to her son, she, like any mother, shows a very practical care. When her son begins to act on his own, this becomes a source of pain for her. She is not permitted to understand all that happens to her immediately but she keeps everything in her heart and continues with blind faith. It is false to think that this development was as if Mary were close to Jesus when he was a child but then clashed with him when he grew up and began his public mission. Rather it is a painful process that is asked of her during the life of her son that includes particularly the passage from faith-filled action to faith-filled suffering.

Through blessing and faith, Mary is linked to Abraham and goes beyond him. She is like him and also greater than him with regard to her relationship with her son. God asked Abraham for his son but did not take him (cf. Gen 22). God asked the son of Mary to walk the path even to death (Lk 22,42). Her son really is taken from Mary. God, who asks more of Mary than of Abraham, gives more to her than to the patriarch. As is shown by her presence in the young Church, Mary can participate in the victory of her son and of his conquering of death. Joy is a characteristic of Mary. In fact the first word that the angel says to her is: "*Rejoice!* " (Lk 1,28). The last words spoken of her in the Gospel of Luke are two blessings (11,27-28). Her personal experience of the relationship with God and with Jesus is in a very particular way one of joy (cf. Lk 1,46-47).

d) John: Mother of Jesus and Mother of his disciples

We have already noted the specific traits that characterise the figure of Mary in John's Gospel: her name "Mary" is never mentioned but the fact that she is the mother of Jesus is stressed. Mary is present at the beginning and the end of Jesus' public ministry. She is not just linked to Jesus but also to the disciples and to people in general. This latter point is significant. Already in Luke's Gospel we have observed that

Chapter VI: Mary in the New Testament

people direct their attention to Mary and are full of admiration for her. A new aspect occurs in John's Gospel where it is seen that Mary is involved in Jesus' relationship to other people, both at the beginning and the end of his ministry. At the marriage feast of Cana, she is concerned about other people, communicates their need to Jesus and directs the people to him. From the cross Jesus binds his mother to the beloved disciple as mother and son. This new reciprocal relationship is determined by Jesus and has its foundation in their personal relationship with him.

John names Mary only with the term "mother". What characterises her is the fact that Jesus received life through her and that in her the Word became flesh (Jn 1,14). Because Jesus has a unique significance for all people who obtain life only through faith in him (Jn,31), Mary, as his mother, has a relationship with everyone.

In Mary and in Jesus the issue is always life. Through Mary, the Son of God enters human life definitively. This fact is a sign of salvation for all people that in our mortal life has appeared the one in whom we receive the fullness of divine life.

The beginning and the end of Jesus' work are connected by means of his "hour". At the beginning, the mother of Jesus is present. She communicates to her son the need of the people. Jesus responds: *"What do you want from me, woman? My hour has not yet come"* (Jn 2,4). The "hour" of Jesus that the Father has determined, the hour of his death, is at the same time the hour of his exaltation (12,23-33; 13,1; 17,1), in which he brings his mission to fulfilment and which will go way beyond people's needs and open to all, access to the life of God. The fact that the hour of Jesus has not yet come does not mean that he cannot or does not want to act, but that his present action is not yet definitive. It is directed towards his "hour" and will be fulfilled only then. Jesus offers wine and joy and is concerned that the feast may continue but this is only a sign of what he will bring about when his hour finally comes.

Also at the end, when Jesus' hour has arrived, his mother is present. Here Jesus no longer offers earthly gifts by a miracle. As a sign that all is fulfilled, from his side pour out blood and water (Jn 19,33-36). From the time that he is exalted, those who believe in him receive the Spirit, who brings life (Jn 7,37-39). When Jesus ends his earthly life and brings his work to fulfilment, his mother is present. She brought him into life and set the scene for the beginning of his ministry. As his mother, Mary has shared in Jesus' life in an intense and personal way. She is the only one who knows the whole life of Jesus. She is a qualified witness to the whole of his life, from the time he was a needy little baby up to his death on the cross.

The public ministry of Jesus began when his mother made the need known to him (Jn 2,3). Jesus brings his public ministry to an end when he turns to his mother and the beloved disciple (Jn 19,26-27). From the crucified Christ, Mary and the disciple receive the task of being for each other mother and son. They do not cease being respectively mother of Jesus and his disciple. Precisely as the mother of Jesus, Mary is the disciple's mother. She symbolises for the disciple the incarnation of the Son of God and his whole mission until its fulfilment. She is a living sign of salvation. She presents to Jesus the needs of the people (Jn 2,3) and directs them to listen to him and put into practice what he tells them (2,5). The way that the disciple reacts to Jesus' mother is described in this way: *"And from that moment the disciple took her into his own"* (Jn 19,27). "His own" is not principally his property and possessions (cf. Jn 1,11-13; 8,44). He is described explicitly as "the disciple whom Jesus loved". What is "his own" above all is therefore his relationship with Jesus: the fact that Jesus loves him and that he believes in Jesus. The disciple introduces Mary into what is his own, that is into his relationship with Jesus. He honours and respects her as the mother of Jesus. Mary gave birth to Jesus and through her he became man and was able to enter into communion with men and women and she points to him, through whom comes life and joy for all people. Therefore she is the mother of Jesus and the mother of his disciples.

Acts of the Apostles: the Mother of Jesus in the Church

In his second work, Luke shows Mary in a new way as belonging to the Church. All those who, after the Ascension of Jesus and following his command, were together in a room in Jerusalem, were there because each had a particular relationship with Jesus. Mary is in this circle as his mother. She is inserted into this community, to which the risen Lord showed himself and which knows that he has entered into the glory of the Father. This community prays with Mary to obtain the Holy Spirit and to know its task to bear witness to Jesus even to the ends of the earth. The Church of all times comes from this community, of which Mary is a living member. The Mother of Jesus belongs to the roots of the Church.

Paul: the Mother of God's Son

The contribution of Paul to the picture of Mary consists in defining in a concise and clear way her role in the history of salvation. Everything comes from God the Father, who desires to save men and women from ruin and allow them to participate in the divine life. For this reason God sent His Son into the world. The task of Mary is to be the mother of the Son of God, who became human by decree of the Father in order to make men and women children of God. Paul does not say any more, nor does he write about the relationship that God and the Son have with Mary, nor how she fulfilled the task given to her.

As regards the way of relating between God, the Son and Mary, Paul certainly offers points of reference and fixes the parameters of the space that can be filled by later theological reflection. How would God, who loves human beings, and the Son of God, who came to save them, act towards the person who is involved in the closest possible way in their plans? In what Paul relates about himself as the servant of Jesus Christ, and regarding God's choice of him and the call that he received from God, he offers us a model to understand what the relationship the maidservant of the Lord has with God.

Chapter VI: Mary in the New Testament

Finally Paul has given us the outline and drawn with a few brief strokes the main characteristics of Mary. We find indications for the later working out of this picture. Paul himself does not, however, elaborate.

The Apocalypse: the Mother as a sign in the heavens

In the vision of Apocalypse 12, the maternal role of Mary has a central place. We contemplate the woman as she is about to give birth. Her son is the king of God's people and the sovereign of all peoples. His place is beside God.

Two aspects of the portrait of Mary come only from this vision: she is threatened by a hostile power and appears as a sign in the heavens. The dragon opposes her, her son and her other children. This dragon is also called *"the ancient serpent, the devil or satan"* (Apoc 12,9) and it seeks to destroy them. The dragon cannot harm the son of the Woman or the Woman herself, as they are under the particular protection of God. The children that follow, however, those that *"observe the commandment of God and are in possession of the testimony of Jesus"* (12,17), are in great anguish. Precisely because of this situation the Woman appears as a great sign in heaven and she is contrasted with the other great sign, the dragon. She shows that everyone must make a choice and a decision and she points the way to God.

2. MARY, THE MOTHER OF THE LORD

In conclusion, let us seek to answer briefly the following questions: what qualities of Mary are at the basis of all the individual traits that we find in the New Testament? What is most characteristic about her?

A response to these questions is possible based on the observations that we have made on all the New Testament passages relating to Mary. Throughout the whole of the New Testament, she is called by her name "Mary" 19 times and 29 times she is called "mother". There are writings in which her proper name does not appear but which present her role as mother (John, Paul, Apocalypse). Normally even where she is named, the fact of her being mother is put in first place. These details are confirmed by the content of the texts. What is most distinctive about Mary is the fact that she is the mother of Jesus. She is not characterised above all by what comes from her, e.g. her faith, but by what comes from God, who chose her as the mother of His Son. Elizabeth mentions in first place the blessing of God, recognising Mary as "*the mother of my Lord*", after which she declares her blessed because of her faith. (Lk 1,42-45).

The motherhood of Mary is the decisive factor and determines how she acts in all her essential relationships: with God, with her son, with people. How God acts towards her and how she responds, correspond to this fundamental reality, that is, that God chose her as the mother of His Son. On her part, Mary believes in the word of God, accepts her task and so becomes the mother of the Lord.

Chapter VI: Mary in the New Testament

For the relationship between Jesus and Mary, fundamental is that they are mother and son. This relationship develops in many ways. How Mary lives this relationship corresponds to the way followed by Jesus, from his conception through to his resurrection. Mary belongs to the people. To them Jesus presents himself with divine authority as he who reveals the will of God and offers a sharing in God's own life. Even though between Jesus and Mary there is a great distance, like that between Creator and creature, and even though Jesus is not only her human son but also her divine Lord, still he remains always her son. To understand how intimate and alive is their relationship goes beyond our capacity. Jesus loves his own to the end (Jn 13,1). The son cannot be outdone in love or in self-giving by the mother.

The relationship between Mary and people is determined by the fact that she is the mother of the Lord. Therefore starting with Elizabeth, countless people have looked to her. Because God has acted within her with creative power, making her the mother of His Son, Mary will be called blessed by all generations. As the mother of Jesus, she must give to the disciple of Jesus her maternal love. The disciple must be included in the relationship between Jesus and Mary. Vice versa, what characterises the disciple, i.e. his relationship with Jesus, must include a relationship with Mary, his mother. She is the mother of the one who has brought his work to completion and gives divine life to men and women. As mother, Mary is bound to Jesus in an inseparable way. For us there remains a never-ending task, to ponder what it means that Mary is the Mother of the Lord, the Mother of God's Son.

Finito di stampare nel mese di settembre 2006
dalla tipografia Città Nuova della P.A.M.O.M.
Via S. Romano in Garfagnana, 23
00148 Roma - tel. 066530467